Mapping Change Management: A Co-Citation Analysis

Air Force Institute of Technology (U.S.). Graduate School of Engineering and Management, Anonymous

MAPPING CHANGE MANAGEMENT:

A CO-CITATION ANALYSIS

THESIS

Brian R. Low, 1st Lieutenant, USAF

AFIT/GEM/ENV/07-M8

DEPARTMENT OF THE AIR FORCE
AIR UNIVERSITY

AIR FORCE INSTITUTE OF TECHNOLOGY

Wright-Patterson Air Force Base, Ohio

AFIT/GEM/ENV/07-M8

MAPPING CHANGE MANAGEMENT:

A CO-CITATION ANALYSIS

THESIS

Presented to the Faculty

Department of Systems and Engineering Management

Graduate School of Engineering and Management

Air Force Institute of Technology

Air University

Air Education and Training Command

In Partial Fulfillment of the Requirements for the

Degree of Master of Science in Engineering and Environmental Management

Brian R. Low, BS

1st Lieutenant, USAF

March 2007

AFIT/GEM/ENV/07-M8

MAPPING CHANGE MANAGEMENT:

A CO-CITATION ANALYSIS

Brian R. Low, BS
1st Lieutenant, USAF

Approved:

/signed/

_____   16 Feb 2007
     Lt Col Daniel Holt (Chairman)   date

/signed/

_____   16 Feb 2007
     Lt Col Summer E. Bartczak (Member)   date

/signed/

_____   16 Feb 2007
  Margaret A. Roach (Member)   date

/signed/

_____   16 Feb 2007
  Sarah V. Hanley (Member)   date

Abstract

Today's organizations are continually undergoing changes to make improvements in their efficiency and effectiveness. The ability for organizations to effectively implement and sustain successful change, however, has been limited, with most change initiatives failing to attain the desired success. To counter this trend, researchers, across several disciplines, have worked to provide practitioners better insight into how to facilitate change within their organizations. This research has developed many theories as to what constitutes change and how best to implement it, but lacks a unifying theory that encompasses all aspects of change research.

This effort took a step in providing a better understanding of the change management field and its nature. By using a co-citation methodology, 141 influential authors from the field of change management were identified. Using quantitative techniques, their works were categorized into identifiable sub-groups within the field and mapped, providing insight into the level of integration that has occurred within the field and across the disciplines that have explored change. Also, the extent that the existing theories have begun to converge toward a unifying theory is observed. The culmination of this effort was to provide future researchers better direction in what research needs to be done, to help the field of change mature towards a unifying theory. This unifying theory can then be translated into successful practices that can enable organizations to successful transition through needed change initiatives.

To my wife and children

Acknowledgments

I would like to express my sincere appreciation to my faculty advisor, Lt Col
Danny Holt, for his guidance and support throughout the course of this thesis effort. The
insight and experience was certainly appreciated. I would, also, like to thank the
members of my committee, and the many librarians for help and support in completing
this endeavor.

Brian R. Low

Table of Contents

List of Figures

List of Tables

MAPPING CHANGE MANAGEMENT – A CO-CITATION ANALYSIS

I. Introduction and Literature Review

Introduction

Organizations today are continually striving to make improvements in their efficiency and effectiveness, introducing frequent structural, process, and human resource initiatives in an effort to change the enterprise and realize gains. Unfortunately, the ability of organizations to effectively implement and sustain change within an organization has not been completely achieved. Beer and Nohria (2000) suggest that 70% of all implemented changes within organizations fail, due to managers not understanding the nature and processes essential to successful change.

Based on this, researchers have attempted to give practitioners some insights into how to better facilitate change within their organizations (Armenakis, Harris, & Mossholder, 1993). Moreover, change research has crossed several academic disciplines where educators, physicians, social and organizational scientists have tried to better understand this phenomenon as they have studied schools, hospitals, societies, and business enterprises. One of the first to tackle organizational change was Lewin (1947), a psychologist, who described the change process in terms of three distinct and sequenced phases, namely, unfreezing, moving, and then freezing once again. In order to help individuals and organizations move through these stages, organizational scientists like Bennis (1969) have encouraged leaders to use comprehensive development and educational strategies to align the beliefs, attitudes, and values of their members with change and development efforts. Moreover, Bennis (1969) and Beer (1976) highlight the need to use the organization's structure and policies to further reinforce change adoption.

These recommendations have been applied and expanded as several researchers have looked at change in specific contexts. Lorenzi and Riley (2000) examined how healthcare organizations integrate and diffuse behavioral and technological changes while Moulding, Silagy and Weller (1999) have offered recommendations to change clinicians' practices by increasing their readiness and reducing the existing barriers against that change. Educators like Waugh and Godfrey (1995) explored how to implement system wide change within a centralized education system where Chauvin and Ellet (1993) and Clarke and James (1996) found that teachers' initial receptivity to change influences adoption and subsequent effectiveness. In sum, the importance of facilitating organizational change, in order to make organizations more responsive to change, has been observed in several different disciplines and contexts.

Van de Ven and Poole (1995) made a concerted effort to integrate the knowledge of change management across several disciplines and contexts. They point out that the many different perspectives on organizational change illustrate contrasting views but can be reduced and integrated into four basic models that describe different types of change and how those types unfold. First, Van de Ven and Poole suggest some changes are imminent, following a logical or natural sequence as the organization ages (i.e., a life-cycle model or process). Second, some changes are goal directed where organizational leaders and members purposefully introduce efforts targeted toward a particular goal or end point. Third, some changes are initiated as power shifts within the organization or the external environment. And, finally, some changes are driven to ensure survival and likened to the evolutionary process that species use to adapt to their environment.

Van de Ven and Poole (1995) argue that efforts to integrate change literature should be pursued as these integration efforts provide greater insight into organizational development. Kuhn (1962) conveys this idea differently in his seminal essay on scientific revolutions. Analogous to Van de Ven and Poole's concept of integration, Kuhn states that fields tend to converge around a set of unifying theories as the field matures. This idea of convergence is familiar to all forms of science, as Kuhn describes research in a particular field of study which builds upon itself until the ideas began to converge into an integrated theory which provides a concentrated basis of study to further the field.

The need for convergence and integration of theories is embedded within the discussions of many fields, including the management sciences. In the field of organizational change specifically, demonstrations of and continual requests for convergence seems to be common. Rajagopalan and Spreitzer (1996) argue that research examining strategic change has focused on one of two areas—the content or the process of strategic change. Those focusing on the content have tested a series of antecedents that lead to change and the consequences of change. Those that focus on the process have typically looked at managers' role in change. The methods used to study each area have differed: content studies have relied on large samples assessing hypotheses with parametric methods while process studies have focused on small longitudinal case studies where data are analyzed qualitatively. Rajagopalan and Spreitzer point that this continued accumulation of differing research contributes little to the field, arguing that these research stresses need to be blended into an overarching theory.

Because little has been done to either understand whether the gain in knowledge from one group (e.g., educators or organizational scientists) has been integrated into a comprehensive theory of organizational change, or to bring convergence to the field of change management as discussed by Rajagopalan and Spreitzer (1996), this project explores this idea of integration and convergence by analyzing the influential research from the field over an extended period of time. Co-citation analysis offers a systematic method in which the field of change management can be studied and categorized.

Co-citation Analysis

The techniques of a co-citation analysis offer insights into the different areas of study within an encompassing field (Cheng, Kumar, Motwani, Reisman, & Madan, 1999; Hoffman & Holbrook, 1993), thereby allowing for a better understanding, and pointing to areas that can be developed further. This method has been applied to the information sciences (Culnan, 1986; White & McCain, 1998) and operations and production management (Pilkington & Liston-Heyes, 1999). In each of these co-citation analyses new insight into the particular academic field was gained. The analyses have demonstrated how fields of study were growing (Cheng et al., 1999), pointed to new areas to be explored (White & Griffith, 1981), and defined new researchers within the field (Culnan, 1986).

This co-citation analysis was conducted first by consulting scholars to obtain either influential papers or authors that have had a significant impact on the field of change management. Using the *Social Sciences Citation Index,* citation and co-citation counts were conducted on the references in order to obtain a co-citation matrix. Statistical analyses were conducted on the co-citation matrix to identify common factors and relationships among the search citations.

Research Questions

Through this analysis of change management, the historical and intellectual structure of the field was charted, providing insights into an integrated theory of organizational change across disciplines in the science of management and differing change theories. Moreover, the analysis illustrated which authors have led the integration effort to make all disciplines better prepared to introduce change in their areas of specialty (Pilkington & Liston-Heyes, 1999). Specifically, the following questions will be addressed: (a) Which authors have significantly impacted the field of change management? (b) What subfields have emerged from within the field of change management? (c) Has the field of change management matured, as evident by its level of convergence? (d) To what extent has research from the different groups (educators, physicians, and organizational scientists) overlapped?

Determining the Maturity of Change Management

The maturity of a field of study can be gauged by studying the reviews conducted by scholars within the field. Reviews are important as they provide a snapshot of the current state of a field of study, pointing out what work has been done to date and providing direction as to where the field should move. When a series of reviews from the same field are studied, a chronology of research starts to appear, pointing to the field's evolution. The study of organizational development and change is no different in this regard. By studying the reviews on change literature some conclusions can be drawn as to how the field has evolved and to what level of maturity it has reached.

An effort was made to find all reviews of organizational change, also included were reviews of organizational development (OD) from which change research originated and which still encompasses the field of organizational change. This was done such that a broad view of the field of change management could be observed. In the end, nine major reviews of organizational development and change where identified. These reviews provided insight into the nature of the field during the time frames specified by the authors and can point to the maturity of the change research during that time frame. Table 1 includes a list of these reviews in chronological order, summarizing the areas of research that the authors specifically covered in the course of their review.

Early Attempts to Structure Change Research

The first review of organizational development was conducted by Friedlander and Brown (1974), which along with identifying what OD research had been done to date, posed the first semblance of structure to the field. Friedlander and Brown reasoned that organizations are composed of people, with differing sets of values, and varied technologies. Organizations are also composed of processes and structures that serve to integrate the people with the technology; this is done to promote both task accomplishment and human fulfillment. Typically, the goal of OD is to optimize human and social development, improve task accomplishment, or some combination of the two. These various goals were categorized by Friedlander and Brown into two approaches by which an organization can improve: "technostructural" or "human-processual" change. Figure 1 illustrates the approach to OD that Friedlander and Brown originally presented.

6

Table 1

List of Organization Development and Change Reviews

Reference	Content – "what" portion of change; research focuses on change factors and types	Context – "where" portion of change; comprises both internal and external environments	Process – "how" change occurs; includes both *descriptive* models and *prescriptive* models that look at stages of change and how to facilitate successful change	Outcome/Consequences – "why" should organizations change; focuses on what goals are attainable	Current Issues/Trends – Reviews then current research, or techniques used in organizational development and change	Theory Development – Discussion on new theory or new settings for OD	Calls for Theory Convergence – Authors stress need for a unifying theory on change
Friedlander & Brown (1974)	■				■		■
Alderfer (1977)					■	■	
Beer & Walton (1987)		■	■			■	
Sashkin & Burke (1987)		■	■			■	
Woodman (1989)	■		■	■	■	■	■
Porras & Silvers (1991)	■		■		■		■
Pasmore & Fagans (1992)			■	■	■		
Barnett & Carroll (1995)	■	■		■			■
Rajagopalan and Spreitzer (1996)	■	■	■	■		■	■
Armenakis & Bedeian (1999)	■			■	■		■

Technostructural Approach to Change

The "technostructural" approach is focused on the relationship between technology which comprises how tasks are accomplished, with the underlining structure of the organization which includes the various relationships and roles of the individuals within the organization (Friedlander & Brown, 1974). Sashkin and Burke (1987) point to the fact that "technostructural" changes are focused on improving task accomplishment or increasing performance. This is done by affecting both the work content and method and also by altering the relationships among workers, resulting in an increased satisfaction with the work environment (Friedlander & Brown, 1974).

Figure 1. Approaches to Organizational Development

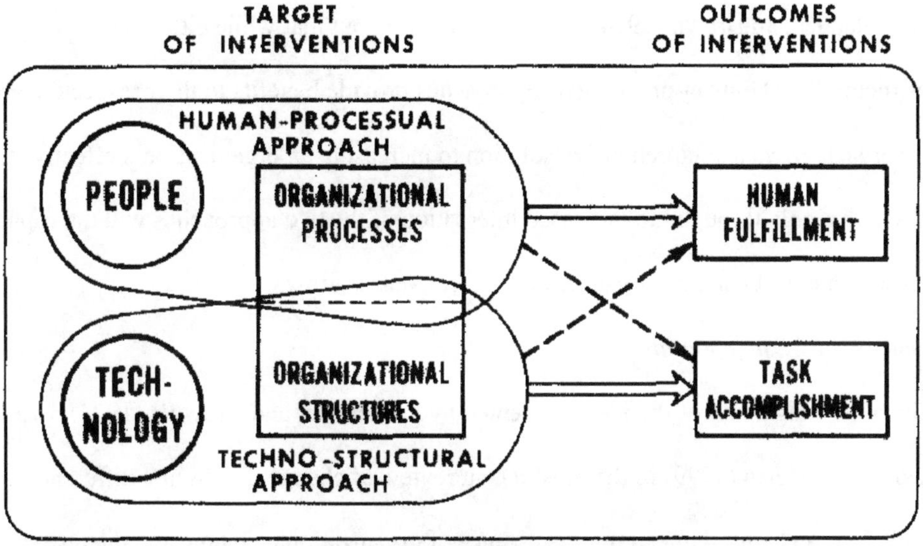

(Friedlander and Brown, 1974)

8

Human-Processual Approach to Change

Friedlander and Brown (1974) describe the "human-processual" approach as one focused on the people within the organization and on how organizational behavioral rooted processes such as communication, problem solving, and decision making can be used to fulfill not only the individual's goals but the organization's as well. The goal of "human-processual" change is the fulfillment of human needs and values (Sashkin & Burke, 1987). With this fulfillment of human needs a corresponding improvement in organizational performance should occur. Unfortunately, Friedlander and Brown point out that while "human-processual" changes have a positive effect on the attitudes of the individuals involved, little evidence was found that a corresponding improvement in either performance or effectiveness occurred.

Friedlander and Brown (1974) were quick to point out that while either the "technostructural" or "human-processual" approaches provide benefits in their respective areas, neither approach offers a comprehensive solution to increasing an organization's effectiveness. They reason that only through the increased integration of the two approaches will the capacity for OD research to influence an organization's effectiveness grow.

A Framework for Change Research

Incorporating many of the ideas presented by Friedlander and Brown's (1974) review, Armenakis and Bedeian (1999) in the most recent review of change highlight a different framework that can be used to capture the essence of organizational change and the research in the field, pointing to the field's increasing evolution. The framework used by Armenakis and Bedeian considers four overarching themes; content, context, processes, and outcomes. Armenakis and Bedeian point out that these themes or issues are common across all organizational changes. This framework will be used as a guide to discuss reviews that were

conducted since Friedlander and Brown's initial piece.

Content

According to Armenakis and Bedeian (1999), content is the "what" aspect of change; it is

here that researchers attempt to quantify what factors will determine whether a change effort is

successful or not. Also, content consists of how change can help an organization. Content

models include Burke and Litwin's (1992) model which looks at transformational and

transactional dimensions of both an individual's and organization's performance and response to

change. Transformational factors presented by Burke and Litwin draw from interactions with

both external and internal environmental forces and require new behavior from the individual

within the organization to cope with the effects of those forces (Burke, 2002). On the other

hand, transactional forces deal more with the smaller, evolutionary growth of an organization

(Burke, 2002). Transactional forces focus on both psychological and organizational values that

influence the culture and performance of an organization (Armenakis & Bedeian, 1999). It is

interesting to note that the Burke-Litwin model highlights the similarities between Friedlander

and Brown's (1974) "technostructural" and "human-processual" approaches and other content

models, pointing to the "what" aspect of change.

While models such as Burke and Litwin (1992) work to explain how change affects an

organization, it is also important to understand the level within the organization that change

should be implemented. Change occurs either at the individual, group, or organizational levels

(Burke, 2002). Woodman (1989) suggests that change research has traditionally focused on the

individual and group levels, without a major focus on changing the whole system. This view corresponds to Porras and Silvers (1991) whose review points to the importance of change beginning at the individual level. They suggest that organizational behavior is affected through individuals changing in response to environmental factors and organizational inputs. While other authors, such as Beer and Walton (1987) and Pasmore and Fagans (1992) suggest that while individual change is important, change must occur at all organizational levels for a change to be institutionalized into the pervading culture.

Another characteristic of content is change type. Most changes fall into one of four categories; these categories are determined by the nature of the change effort, whether it was planned or unexpected, and by the scope of the change, whether it is incremental or dramatic in nature. As Porras and Robertson (1992) discuss the differences in the types of change, they point out that planned change is a deliberate act by the organization to improve itself, while unplanned change occurs when the organization is forced to respond to some unexpected outside force. In further explanation, Porras and Robertson define incremental change as "continuous improvement" which occurs when the organization undergoes many small changes without altering the overarching structure, eventually shifting the system to some new form. Opposite this are dramatic changes, which are fundamental shifts that transform the organization to a new form by passing the small steps used in incremental change (Porras & Robertson, 1992, Burke, 2002). Table 2 shows how both the scope and nature of change result in different change forms.

Context

Armenakis and Bedeian (1999) defined the context of change as the "where" aspect, focusing on both the external and internal environments where the change effort is being undertaken. Researchers point to the fact that all human organizations are essentially open

systems (Beer & Walton, 1987, Burke, 2002). Constant interaction with

Table 2

Types of Organizational Change

Scope of Change	Nature of Change	
	Planned	Unplanned
Incremental change	Developmental	Evolutionary
Dramatic change	Transformational	Revolutionary

(Porras and Robertson, 1992)

their surrounding environment is essential for their survival. This environment provides energy

(money, raw materials, and people) that is then used internally and converted into some form of

output (Burke, 2002). But just as the external environment provides opportunities, it also places

constraints that can affect organizational change such as market characteristics and governmental

regulations. How an organization exists within this external environment plays a large part on

how the organization will act, how it will evolve and how it will change. Along with external

factors, internal environment considerations are just as important. Barnett and Carroll (1995) in

their review stress the importance of internal environments by pointing to such internal factors as

organization size, age, and composition which are important factors in an organization's ability

to change. While these internal factors can be used as a foundation for successful change, they

can also prove detrimental in change initiatives. Barnett and Carroll cite factors such as

organization age and size which can lead to an increase in bureaucracy resulting in less inertia in the organization and would constitute a hurdle to change (Hannan & Freeman, 1984). Understanding these environmental forces is essential in conducting organizational change, as they can greatly affect the outcome of that change.

Process

The idea of "how" an organization goes about change is covered under the theme of process research. There has been a considerable amount of research done trying to show the best method for an organization to successfully implement change. Research conducted here typically falls into two categories: models that describe how change takes place – *descriptive models,* and those models that attempt to give direction in guiding change through an organization – *prescriptive models.*

Most descriptive models stem from Lewin's (1947) work in describing how an organization undergoes change. Lewin pointed to three distinct stages that the organization would pass through; unfreezing, moving, and refreezing. The first stage, unfreezing, is where the organization is prepared to change. Next the organization will undergo the actual change, which consists of moving to a new state. Finally, the organization will refreeze or adopt the change into the organization's culture. Later descriptive models all followed this basic outline in how an organization will change. Some models provide more in-depth steps that further described the change process, such as Armenakis, Harris and Feild (1999) which added a commitment stage pointing to the acceptance necessary for an organization to adopt a change initiative. In the end, all of these different theories provide organizations with a road map for change; they illustrate what steps the organization must take for a change initiative to be adopted within their organization.

While the understanding of what steps are necessary for change to take place is important, it is equally vital that the right information and techniques are used to help an organization move through those steps. Prescriptive theories point to what is necessary for the process to take place. They speak to the importance of creating a sense of ownership by increasing readiness and individual participation in the change effort (Pasmore & Fagans, 1992, Porras & Silvers, 1991). Most theories identify two factors that are essential to successful change; they consist of the change message and how that message is delivered. Armenakis et al. (1999) developed a prescriptive model that embodies this idea. In their model, Armenakis et al. stress that the change message is at the core of successfully preparing an organization to accept a change initiative. They call for five components to be included in any change message; *discrepancy* – which answers the question of "is the change necessary," *appropriateness* – which confirms that the change is the right one to meet the discrepancy, *efficacy* – which provides the confidence that the change can be implemented successfully, *principle support* – which lets members of the organization know that their leadership is behind the change, and finally *personal valence* – which lets the members of the organization know how they will benefit from the change. The ability for members of the organization to receive adequate answers to their questions concerning the change initiative will determine how committed they become to accepting the planned change.

Along with the importance of what is conveyed by the change message, the strategies employed to deliver the message will determine how accepting members of the organization are to the upcoming change. Armenakis et al. (1999) suggest several strategies such as: *active participation, diffusion practices, formalization practices, rites & ceremonies, persuasive communication, human resource management practices, and information management,* that when properly used can help to successfully communicate and reinforce the change message.

Outcomes

Equally as important as answering the questions of "what," "where," and "how" to change, researchers have asked the question of "why." The outcome of change is an important facet to organizations considering a new initiative that requires change. There must be some benefit for the organization to go through the change process or the effort is wasted. Researchers have worked to define a change initiative's possible outcomes, such that organizations can measure the affect of change upon itself.

Change initiatives typically start with some goal in mind (Van de Ven & Poole, 1995) and some way to measure success (or failure) such as profitability or market share (Armenakis & Bedeian, 1999, Porras & Silvers, 1991, Rajagopalan & Spreitzer, 1996). While profitability or market share are an easy way to measure and gauge the change initiative's successfulness, other goals or outcomes are harder to measure. In contrast to performance gains, individual development and individual self-actualization can also be desired outcomes of organizational change (Porras & Silvers, 1991).

Organizational change will often work to increase factors such as operational effectiveness or performance, but can in turn lead to some unintended response such as increased resistance, which then can promote a feeling of stress or cynicism resulting in reduced organizational performance (Armenakis & Bedeian, 1999). The ability to successfully measure these content or contextual factors is also an important gauge in the successfulness of a change.

The ability to successfully monitor and measure these content or contextual issues is also of importance to researchers, as it provides insight into what is happening throughout the change initiative. Barnett and Carroll (1995) point to the importance of measuring change at the organizational level as it provides information that contributes to organizational theory; they also speak to insuring that measured outcomes are applicable. Often the factors that are measured are insufficient to allow broad comparisons among different types of organizations which can contribute to the growth of new theory.

Need to Integrate Research

The preceding issues point to where most of the current research in organizational change is being conducted. However, while individual research efforts will fall into one of the categories listed above, Armenakis and Bedeian (1999) point out that generally organizational change research is limited in scope as it focuses on only one aspect of change. They call for a need to integrate the different streams of change research, thus unifying the field of organizational change, giving researchers a better ability to predict how and why organizations change. Armenakis and Bedeian are not alone in their recent calls for further integration of the field of change management; Barnett and Carroll (1995) suggest that theories on organizational change should include both content and process elements, yet conclude that current theories are often one dimensional, either of a content or process mindset.

This call for integrating the different aspects of change research has existed since the first attempts to review and quantify the field of organizational development and change. As noted, Friedlander and Brown (1974) made calls not only for the convergence and integration of the various research methods in use for studying OD, but also called for an incorporation of knowledge from the different streams of research being done within OD. Friedlander and Brown

suggested that work should be done toward a general theory of planned change that would look

outside the narrow range of research that had been done to that date. As evident by similar calls

from Barnett and Carroll (1995), Rajagopalan and Spreitzer (1996), and Armenakis and Bedeian

(1999) almost three decades after Friedlander and Brown, the field of change management is still

calling for a unifying effort that will link the various streams of research into one general change

theory that incorporates both the content and process along with the context of change.

Woodman (1989) said it best as he discussed the need for a more comprehensive framework or

model of change among the many existing theories: "we have plenty of theories; what the field

[change management] needs is more theorists – or at least, more effort by theorists to integrate

existing knowledge." (p. 211)

Convergence

So what is convergence, and how does it occur? At its basis, research in a field is built on

previous work that the scientific community has accepted as the conceptual and methodological

foundation of a particular field. Convergence comes as the intellectual field matures such that a

set of theories, models, methods (to include measures) emerge and are accepted, serving as a

guide to subsequent research.

In his essay on how sciences develop, Kuhn (1962) discusses the progression through

which most fields of science evolve and how they eventually go through the process of

convergence. Most fields of science have stemmed from one idea or hypothesis. That

hypothesis is then tested and when deemed more robust through empirical tests becomes a

working theory. Once a founding theory has been established, different scientists and researchers will draw their own conclusions and theories based on their understanding of the concepts and on their research goals. This wide body of theories, while together are similar in content, individually are often very different in content and scope. Over a period of time this body of theories is further refined, with additional researchers building on the work of their predecessors, selecting the pieces that are most relevant. This refinement process is continuously occurring as the field matures until eventually the research and theories began to converge into some form of unifying thought. This convergence of theories leads to what Kuhn called "paradigms" which he describes as ideas or theories that while they are unprecedented enough to attract a group of followers, they are still open-ended such that they still leave problems that need to be redefined by further research. This process of scientific evolution is illustrated in Figure 2.

The idea of forming "paradigms" or unifying different theories into one cohesive idea defines the maturity of a field of study. It provides a unifying effort for researchers in the field, while still providing enough unanswered questions that further research is needed. Kuhn points to this fact by suggesting that paradigms are not constant, the process of scientific development continues by replacing the old paradigms with new as the body of research evolves.

Summary

The continual calls for convergence from the first review of organizational development (Friedlander and Brown, 1974) up to and including the most recent review (Armenakis and Bedeian, 1999) suggest that organizational change has not evolved to the point of having one unifying theory or paradigm. To help this happen it is important to understand the nature and make-up of the field today. This will lead to a better understanding of what divergent theories exist and how they can be incorporated together and refined, such that they can be converged to

create a unifying theory. The following

Figure 2. Development of Science

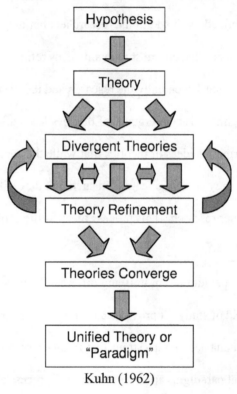

Kuhn (1962)

chapters will detail an attempt to categorize and map the field of change management

quantitatively using a co-citation analysis. The resulting analysis will provide insight into how

change research is grouped; also hopefully patterns will be evident pointing to not only theory

refinement, but convergence of those theories.

II. Method

Phase I—Identification of Influential Authors

Author co-citation analysis begins with the selection of authors and manuscripts to be searched as cited references. While some studies begin with a predetermined list of authors and manuscripts (H. D. White & Griffith, 1981), no *a priori* list was developed for this study. Instead, the advice of a group of scholars was sought to assist in the identification of authors and manuscripts so that the first research question could be addressed (i.e., which authors have significantly impacted the field of change management?); a complete list of those contacted is presented in Appendix A. The researchers that were consulted were those that have authored review articles in the discipline of organizational change and development in the last decade. These reviews have appeared in the *Annual Review of Psychology* (1996-2005), *Academy of Management Review (1996-2005), Journal of Management* (1996-2005), and *Journal of Applied Psychology (1996-2005)*. In addition, editors of leading management journals that publish change-related manuscripts were consulted. These included: *Academy of Management Review, Administrative Science Quarterly, Annual Review of Psychology, Industrial and Corporate Change, The Journal of Applied Behavioral Science, Journal of Applied Psychology, Journal of Change Management, Journal of Management, Journal of Organizational Change Management, Journal of Strategic Change and Development, Leadership & Organization Development Journal, and Research in Organizational Change*. Finally, authors writing change-related manuscripts in these leading journals were contacted. These authors were identified using various databases (e.g., ABI/Inform, Compendex, and ArticleFirst) along with manual searches.

This consultant group was contacted through a personalized electronic mail message. The message asked each individual to nominate the most influential authors, manuscripts, and journals in the field of organizational change and development. In addition to the request for specific information, the message described the purpose and background of the study. This method provided several advantages. First, a large group of authors' and editors' opinions could be garnered rather quickly, providing a valid list of influential authors to use as a basis for the co-citation analysis. In addition, it overcomes potential shortcomings that might arise because of the researcher's inexperience with the discipline. It is important to note that there was still a possibility of bias as these authors' and editors' opinions were solicited. Bias could be introduced in several ways. For instance, the individuals' editorial and publishing history might influence the list of journals that are identified where individuals would be expected to favor those journals that they have edited or contributed to as an author.

In all, 58 scholars were sent personalized messages. In addition, two types of follow-ups were sent to specific scholars. First, a basic reminder and request was sent to those that had not responded to the first messages and those that had indicated that they were out of the office and could not respond at that time. Second, a message was sent to the journal editors that declined to provide any information because organizational development and change was not their primary discipline of study. Assuming these editors had a list of reviewers that they considered experts in the discipline, this message asked that they provide the names of a few scholars who reviewed manuscripts in the discipline organizational change and development. The findings and the names that these experts provided are discussed in the results.

Phase II – Citation and Co-citation Search

Using the results from Phase I, the citation and co-citation searches were conducted in a fashion similar to what Culnan (1986) describes in her study of the management information systems literature. This required four basic steps that included: (a) a citation search (of authors or manuscripts); (b) narrowing the data pool of authors or manuscripts, focusing on the most salient; (c) a co-citation search of the most salient data; and (d) a statistical analysis of the data (discussed in the subsequent section). Consistent with Culnan (1986), the citation and co-citation analyses were conducted using *Social Sciences Citation Index (SSCI)*. The *SSCI* includes bibliographic information, abstracts, and cited references for manuscripts published in more than 5,000 scholarly journals, representing more than 50 disciplines (Thomson Scientific, 2006). Specifically, the *SSCI* includes journals related to education, health services, and management. Thus, the *SSCI* reflects the diversity observed in the change literature.

As noted, the pool of authors identified in Phase I was used to conduct the initial citation search. By using a particular author's name as a search term in the *SSCI* database, documents that have referenced the author over the specified time period were identified. From this, an initial citation count for each author was obtained. In addition, the extent to which specific documents that were identified in Phase I are cited was explored. However, this posed several challenges. Culnan (1986) and White and Griffith (1981) point out that it is difficult to search for individual documents for theoretical and technical reasons. Theoretically, in a co-citation search the documents or authors selected are to represent the body of knowledge that the particular author has added to the field. When authors' names are used as the basis of the cited reference search, the broader is the body of knowledge that is represented by capturing all of the papers written by the individual author. In contrast, when searches are restricted to only one document, the body of work that is captured is limited to only one document. Also technically, the way that *SSCI* catalogs and indexes documents presents challenges. *SSCI* documents are cataloged by publication year, journal code, volume, issue number, and page number. Because of this, searches require far more information and often return inaccurate results (Culnan, 1986; H. D. White & Griffith, 1981).

In order to further narrow the pool of authors to those that are most influential, authors that are cited by fewer than 30 sources were removed from the subsequent searches and analyses. This cutoff was used based on the recommendations offered by Culnan (1986), who developed this standard through personal discussions with Belver Griffith, one of the developers of the co-citation analysis technique (see White & Griffith (1981), for a general description of the method). Culnan reasoned that the probability of identifying a set of authors that are jointly cited increases significantly with greater individual citation counts Thus, the ability of the research project to fulfill its fundamental objectives of identifying authors that have significantly impacted the field of change management, discerning recognizable subfields within the body of change research and observing the extent of research overlap and theory convergence is reduced.

Using the narrowed pool of authors and documents, a second *SSCI* search was conducted to identify the number of times two individual authors were co-cited in a document. Individual citation searches were combined using Boolean operators (e.g., and) so all manuscripts could be identified that cite each author pair over the specified time periods. This co-citation search yielded a matrix that contains the counts for each pair searched.

In addition, this data was used to identify the relative importance of each author within the field of change management by computing the diagonals of each author. This is done by summing the three highest intersections and dividing by two (Culnan, 1986; H. D. White & Griffith, 1981). This procedure is done such that errors associated with inflated results can be accounted for when determining relative importance to the field. Due to limitations in the search algorithms used in the *SSCI* database, when a cited reference search is conducted on an author name the returned results include all possible authors by the given name. Whenever possible, first and middle initials were used to identify the specific author being searched; however, this is insufficient on some occasions when two or more authors may share not only last names but initials as well. As typically only authors in related fields will be co-cited within a paper, co-citation counts eliminate the inflation in single citation counts caused by authors not writing in the field of change management. This provides a basis to use co-citation data as a determining factor in assessing an author's importance in a field. At this point, the matrix of co-citation counts was used for further statistical analysis that addressed the remaining research questions. This is described in the following section.

Phase III – Statistical Analysis

To identify the subfields of organizational change and development research that have emerged, a factor analysis was conducted on the matrix of co-citation counts that was obtained (Culnan, 1986). The factor analysis was conducted using the methods prescribed by Conway and Huffcutt (2003), and Ford, MacCallum, and Tait (1986).

Thus, the items were factor analyzed using the principle axis method and a varimax rotation and the number of factors that were retained was based on an interpretation of the eigenvalue criterion in conjunction with a scree plot. Generally, factor analysis is a means to reduce a set of observations to a smaller set of factors that capture the overlap and similarities between the unique observations (Pilkington & Liston-Heyes, 1999). In this particular setting, the purpose is not different; the factor analysis was able to reduce the matrix of co-citations into a smaller set that highlighted those authors and documents that were typically cited together. The identified factors were analyzed in order to identify common research themes among the authors loaded on each factor, such that the factors can be named. The documents that have been written by those authors on each factor were identified (using SSCI) so that the contents of these documents could be studied to identify common themes within the manuscripts. Also, documents that co-cited authors on each factor were studied to ensure that the common themes identified in the author's papers were consistent throughout the factor. This is done under the assumption that authors that are co-cited repeatedly share a common research theme.

To pictorially represent these themes (Kachigan, 1991), a multidimensional scaling analysis (MDS) was conducted from the co-citation matrix that was generated in Phase II (Culnan, 1986). The MDS is done by converting the raw co-citation counts from the matrix developed in Phase II and factor analyzed in Phase III into a matrix of bivariate correlations. Beyond the ability to identify author groups within the body of literature (which is done with the factor analysis described), White and Griffith (1981) give additional reasons to create a MDS map of co-citation data. These include: (a) the locations of these groups with respect to each other; (b) the relative centrality and peripherality of each author or document within the different groups and with respect to the overall field; (c) proximities of authors or documents within groups and across the different group boundaries; and (d) the position with respect to the map's axes of each author or document.

III. Results

Phase I - Identification of authors

The first phase of the project was designed to identify those authors and manuscripts that have significantly impacted the field of change management. Twenty-two of the 58 scholars initially contacted responded with the requested information, 21 others responded but declined to provide any information (largely journal editors indicating that organizational development and change was not their primary discipline of study), and finally, nine messages were returned undelivered (chiefly those with foreign email accounts). Those that responded were encouraging and eager to provide helpful information. They provided a list of 69 influential authors, eight key papers, and 20 journals. Moreover, they included 13 influential change and development books and book series. Table 3 summarizes the responses provided by the experts. Responses suggested that the subsequent analysis should focus on influential authors rather than specific manuscripts or journals. Even when the scholars specified a paper or journal they were typically stating that it was a source of additional authors. When all of these were considered, a list of 138 authors emerged and this list was used as the basis for the study.

Using this author-focused recommendation, the list was reviewed to insure a broad coverage of change literature. The list was then supplemented with 22 additional authors to include those experts that were involved in the initial identification of authors to help provide a broad coverage of the field of change management. After deleting redundant authors, a list of 141 authors was used as the basis of the subsequent steps. The final list of authors used in the citation analysis is shown in Table 4.

Table 3.

Information Returned from Solicited Scholars

Influential Authors

Adler, N	Ford, JD	Lawler, EE	Reger, R
Alvesson, M	Francis, D	Lawrence	Ritzer, G
Argyris, C	French, J	Ledford, GE	Robert HM
Armenakis, A	French, W	Lewin, K	Romanelli, E
Bandura, A	Galbraith, JR	Lorsch, JW	Rousseau, D
Barr, PS	Gersick, CG	Markegard, B	Sashkin, M
Bartlett, CA	Ghoshal, S	Martin, R	Schaffer, RH
Bartunek, D	Goldsmith, HM	Mathews, J	Schein, E
Bartunek, J	Golembiewski, R	Mauborgne, R	Senge, PM
Beckhard, R	Goodstein, L	Meyer, J	Shani, R
Bedeian, A	Gray, B	Miliken, FJ	Shortell, SM
Beer, M	Greenwood, R	Mindrum, C	Spier, M
Beer, S	Greiner, L	Mirvis, P	Sprietzer, G
Benne, KD	Greve, MS	Moore, L	Sproull, LS
Bennis, W	Hage, JT	Morley, E	Stacey, RD
Bentein, K	Harris, R	Morrison, EW	Stevenson, W
Blake, RR	Harrison, R	Mouton, JS	Stewart, W
Boeker, W	Heneman, RL	Neill, T	Stimpert, JL
Bower, JL	Hersey, P	Nelson	Sundstrom, K
Bradford	Hirschhorn, L	Nohria, N	Tannenbaum
Brown, D	Hooper, A	Oreg, S	Tsoukas, H
Burke, W	Hornstein, H	O'Reilly, C	Tushman, M
Bushe, G	Hough, J	Oshry, B	Van de Ven, A
Carlson, H	Huff	Oshry, KE	van Dick, R
Coch, L	Huy, QN	Palmer, I	Walton, RE
Cohen, AR	Jensen, MC	Pasmore, W	Weick, KE
Conger, JA	Johnson, J	Pettigrew, AM	White, M
Cooperrider, D	Jones, J	Poole, MS	Williams, P
Cummings, T	Kakabadse, A	Porras, J	Winter
Daft, RL	Kakabadse, N	Potter, J	Woodcock, M
Davis	Kanter, RM	Powell, WW	Woodman, R
DiMaggio, P	Kiesler	Prasad, P	Worley, CG
Dunphy, D	Kim, WC	Quinn, R	Wruck, KH
Eddy, W	Kotter, J	Rajagopalan, N	Zajac, EJ
Ferguson	Langley, A		

Influential Manuscripts

"Biography of an Institution" (Bradford, 1967)

"Contextual research and the study of organizational change processes" (Pettigrew, 1985)

"From individual to team to cadre: tracking leadership for the third millennium" (Kakabadse, 2000)

"Making modernising government initiative work: A culture change through collaborative inquiry" (Kakabadse and Kakabadse, 2002)

Table 3 (Cont.)

Influential Manuscripts (Cont.)

"Symbolic process in the implementation of technological change: A symbolic interactionist study of work computerization" (Prasad, 1993)

"T-group movement" (Fesler, 1970)

"The practical theorist: the life and work of Kurt Lewin" (Marrow, 1969)

"Tipping point leadership" (Kim and Mauborgne, 2003)

Influential Journals

Academy of Management Journal

Academy of Management Review

Action Research

Administrative Science Quarterly

American Journal of Sociology

American Sociological Review

Appreciative Inquiry

Harvard Business Review on Change

Human Relations

Journal of Applied Behavioral Science

Journal of Applied Psychology

Journal of Management

Journal of Organizational Change Management

Organization Science

Organizational Development Journal

Organizational Dynamics

Pubilc Administration and Development

Strategic Change

Strategic Management Journal

Influential Books and Book Series

A force for change (Kotter, 1990)

An invented life: reflections on leadership and change (Bennis, 1993)

Breaking the code of change (Beer and Nohria, 2000)

Creating futures: leading change through information systems (Kakabadse and Kakabadse, 2000)

Intelligent leadership: Creating a passion for change (Hooper and Potter, 2000)

Organization change: Theory and practice (Burke, 2002)

Organization development and change (Cummings and Worley, 2004)

Organization development series (Schein, Bennis and Beckhard, 1969)

Organizations evolving (Aldrich, 2001)

Research in organizational change and development series (Passmore and Woodman (Eds.))

The Civil Service: Continuity and change (Office, 1994)

The evolution of cooperation (Axelrod, 1997)

The tools of change: New technology and the democratisation of work (Mathews, 1989)

Table 4.

Authors Used in Co-citation Search

Adler, NJ	Ford, JD	Kotter, J	Quinn, RW
Alvesson, M	Francis, D	Langley, A	Rajagopalan, N
Argyris, C	French, JL	Lawler, EE	Reger, R
Armenakis, AA	French, W	Lawrence, PR	Romanelli, E
Bandura, A	Galbraith, JR	Ledford, GE	Rousseau, DM
Barr, PS	Gersick, CG	Lewin, K	Sashkin, M
Bartlett, CA	Ghoshal, S	Lorsch, JW	Schaffer, RH
Bartunek, D	Ginsburg, LR	Markegard, B	Schein, E
Bartunek, J	Goldsmith, HM	Martin, R	Sebastian, JG
Beckhard, R	Golembiewski, RT	Mathews, J	Senge, PM
Bedeian, A	Goodstein, LD	Mauborgne, R	Shani, R
Beer, M	Gray, B	Miliken, FJ	Shortell, SM
Beer, S	Greenwood, R	Miller, RH	Spier, M
Benne, KD	Greiner, L	Mindrum, C	Sprietzer, G
Bennis, W	Greve, MS	Mirvis, P	Sproull, LS
Bentein, K	Hage, JT	Moore, L	Stacey, RD
Blake, RR	Harris, RT	Morley, E	Stevenson, WB
Boeker, W	Harrison, R	Morrison, EW	Stewart, WH
Bower, JL	Heneman, RL	Mouton, JS	Stimpert, JL
Bradford	Hersey, P	Neill, T	Sundstrom, K
Brown, LD	Hirschhorn, L	Nelson, RR	Tannenbaum, R
Burke, WW	Hooper, A	Nohria, N	Tregunno, D
Bushe, G	Hornstein, H	Oreg, S	Tsoukas, H
Carlson, H	Hough, JR	O'Reilly, C	Tushman, M
Coch, L	Huff, AS	Oshry, B	Van de Ven, AH
Cohen, AR	Huff, JO	Oshry, KE	van Dick, R
Conger, JA	Huy, QN	Palmer, I	Walton, RE
Cooperrider, D	Jensen, MC	Pasmore, WA	Weick, KE
Cummings, TG	Johnson, J	Pettigrew, AM	White, MC
Daft, RL	Jones, J	Poole, MS	Winter, SG
Davis, DA	Kakabadse, A	Porras, JI	Woodcock, M
DiClemente, CC	Kakabadse, N	Potter, J	Woodman, R
DiMaggio, P	Kanter, RM	Powell, WW	Worley, CG
Dunphy, D	Kiesler, S	Prasad, P	Wruck, KH
Eddy, W	Kim, WC	Prochaska, JO	Zajac, EJ

Phase II – Citation and Co-citation search

Single author citation counts for each of the authors identified in Phase I were conducted using the *SSCI* database. Author citation counts ranged from a high of 24,418 for Albert Bandura to lows of zero for several authors (e.g., Johnson, J.). The five authors with the most single citation counts were: Bandura (24,418), Jensen (7,104),

30

Prochaska (6,321), Kanter (6,192), and Weick (5,573). Across all of the 141 authors that were explored, the average count was 1,202. While the average citation counts appeared substantial, these counts may still be an underestimate of the totals because the *SSCI* database contained only those articles that had been published from 1980 to the present. The full results of the initial citation search in rank order are shown in Table 5.

After eliminating those authors that had been cited fewer than 30 times (see the discussion in the method), co-citation searches were conducted. The co-citation matrix with all authors is presented in Appendix B. The diagonals for each author were computed from the matrix using the method described by White and Griffith (1981). This value was computed by summing the three largest intersections for each author and dividing by two. There was a considerable range between the diagonals of the authors searched; Prochaska had the largest diagonal at 2,827, while the lowest was Harris with 2.5. The five largest diagonals were: Prochaska (2,827), DiClemente (2,677.5), Bandura (1,783.5), Powell (1,641.5), and DiMaggio (1,541). The diagonals for all of the authors studied can be found in Table 6.

It is important to note that importance of an author in the field can not be determined by single author's citation counts alone. Because of the limitations in the *SSCI* database search algorithm, when a cited author was searched, all authors by that name were returned. In some cases several authors were returned and the number representing the author's citation count was actually the combined total of all of the returned authors; regardless of the discipline. The co-citation search and subsequent diagonal computation was done to help minimize the possibility of this error from occurring.

Table 5.

Rank Order of Single Citation Counts

Rank Order	Author	Single Citation Count	Rank Order	Author	Single Citation Count
1	Bandura, A	24,418	72	Reger, R	469
2	Jensen, MC	7,104	73	Cummings, TG	463
3	Prochaska, JO	6,321	74	Sashkin, M	404
4	Kanter, RM	6,192	75	Dunphy, D	401
5	Weick, KE	5,573	76	Sproull, LS	388
6	Lewin, K	5,502	77	Beckhard, R	387
7	Nelson, RR	5,476	78	Goodstein, LD	380
8	DiClemente, CC	5,069	79	Armenakis, AA	380
9	Argyris, C	5,032	80	Langley, A	343
10	Schein, E	4,525	81	Coch, L	307
11	Powell, WW	4,073	82	Prasad, P	298
12	DiMaggio, P	3,946	83	Hornstein, H	292
13	O'Reilly, C	3,317	84	Stacey, RD	287
14	Lawler, EE	3,270	85	Ledford, GE	286
15	Tushman, M	2,921	86	Heneman, RL	275
16	Potter, J	2,820	87	Burke, WW	275
17	Van de Ven, AH	2,816	88	Porras, JI	269
18	Daft, RL	2,786	89	Tannenbaum, R	256
19	Lawrence, PR	2,552	90	Rajagopalan, N	214
20	Shortell, SM	2,293	91	Mauborgne, R	208
21	Rousseau, D	2,267	92	French, JL	202
22	Kiesler, S	2,256	93	Stimpert, JL	199
23	Greenwood, R	2,008	94	Pasmore, WA	196
24	Bennis, W	1,958	95	Benne, KD	190
25	Kotter, J	1,753	96	Stewart, WH	164
26	Senge, PM	1,680	97	Barr, PS	157
27	Galbraith, JR	1,635	98	Cooperrider, D	156
28	Walton, RE	1,587	99	Stevenson, WB	155
29	Pettigrew, AM	1,581	100	Greve, MS	137
30	Ghoshal, S	1,534	101	Schaffer, RH	123
31	Gray, B	1,527	102	Kakabadse, A	121
32	Brown, LD	1,385	103	Harris, RT	120
33	Morrison, EW	1,337	104	van Dick, R	109
34	Miller, RH	1,315	105	Bushe, G	92
35	Alvesson, M	1,197	106	Mouton, JS	82
36	Beer, S	1,185	107	Huy, QN	74
37	Nohria, N	1,183	108	Sebastian, JG	63
38	Harrison, Roger	1,183	109	Quinn, RW	42
39	Zajac, EJ	1,169	110	Hough, JR	41
40	Bartlett, CA	1,167	111	Shani, R	33
41	Winter, SG	1,135	112	Kakabadse, N*	27
42	Poole, MS	1,125	113	Oshry, B*	25
43	Bedeian, A	1,116	114	Neill, T*	23
44	Beer, M	1,064	115	Hage, JT*	21

Table 5 (Cont.)

Rank Order of Single Citation Counts (Cont.)

Rank Order	Author	Single Citation Count	Rank Order	Author	Single Citation Count
45	Adler, NJ	1,026	116	Woodcock, M*	20
46	Blake, RR	1,024	117	Bentein, K*	17
47	Davis, DA	938	118	Morley, E*	12
48	Golembiewski, RT	936	119	Worley, CG*	12
49	Greiner, L	902	120	Miliken, FJ*	11
50	Bower, JL	902	121	Carlson, H*	8
51	French, W	887	122	Oreg, S*	7
52	Ford, JD	828	123	Gersick, CG*	5
53	Moore, L	811	124	Goldsmith, HM*	4
54	Conger, JA	808	125	Bartunek, D*	0
55	Hirschhorn, L	705	126	Bradford*	0
56	Eddy, W	678	127	Ferguson*	0
57	Hersey, P	647	128	Francis, D*	0
58	Huff, AS	634	129	Ginsburg, LR*	0
59	Kim, WC	626	130	Hooper, A*	0
60	Bartunek, J	621	131	Huff, JO*	0
61	Mathews, J	613	132	Johnson, J*	0
62	Tsoukas, H	572	133	Jones, J*	0
63	Lorsch, JW	568	134	Markegard, B*	0
64	Mirvis, P	554	135	Martin, R*	0
65	Woodman, R	551	136	Mindrum, C*	0
66	Boeker, W	546	137	Oshry, KE*	0
67	Romanelli, E	544	138	Spier, M*	0
68	Wruck, KH	513	139	Sprietzer, G*	0
69	Palmer, I	512	140	Sundstrom, K*	0
70	White, MC	478	141	Tregunno, D*	0
71	Cohen, AR	475			

Note. * Indicates authors that were removed from the subsequent co-citation search due to insufficient single citations.

Table 6.

Rank Order of Average Largest Co-citation Intersections

Rank	Author	Largest Citation Counts			Total
		1	2	3	
1	Prochaska, JO	3976	1620	58	2827
2	DiClemente, CC	3976	1336	43	2677.5
3	Bandura, A	1620	1336	611	1783.5
4	Powell, WW	2293	531	459	1641.5
5	DiMaggio, P	2293	473	316	1541
6	Weick, KE	970	644	583	1098.5
7	Argyris, C	773	644	486	951.5
8	Daft, RL	970	474	416	930
9	Schein, E	773	573	506	926
10	Tushman, M	583	569	546	849
11	Nelson, RR	628	546	438	806
12	Van de Ven, AH	569	553	459	790.5
13	Kanter, RM	506	461	445	706
14	Lawrence, PR	502	459	378	669.5
15	Lewin, K	611	389	338	669
16	Galbraith, JR	459	405	354	609
17	Rousseau, D	323	322	546	595.5
18	Ghoshal, S	597	330	242	584.5
19	O'Reilly, C	445	360	343	574
20	Pettigrew, AM	408	287	267	481
21	Bartlett, CA	597	231	130	479
22	Senge, PM	486	244	223	476.5
23	Winter, SG	628	156	134	459
24	Nohria, N	336	330	231	448.5
25	Jensen, MC	324	296	247	433.5
26	Zajac, EJ	296	287	275	429
27	Kiesler, S	375	235	228	419
28	Kotter, J	352	267	216	417.5
29	Bennis, W	306	290	234	415
30	Lawler, EE	286	270	251	403.5
31	Poole, MS	303	246	215	382
32	Greenwood, R	251	243	204	349
33	Shortell, SM	287	236	161	342
34	Romanelli, E	425	130	119	337
35	Huff, AS	254	200	128	291
36	Alvesson, M	231	164	119	257
37	Bower, JL	220	148	133	250.5
38	Walton, RE	214	144	141	249.5
39	Bartunek, J	207	157	130	247
40	Boeker, W	179	175	134	244
41	Morrison, EW	202	139	114	227.5
42	Beer, M	159	157	134	225
43	Gray, B	152	149	133	217
44	Kim, WC	208	116	97	210.5
45	Conger, JA	151	141	129	210.5

Table 6 (Cont.)

Rank Order of Average Largest Co-citation Intersections (Cont.)

| Rank | Author | Largest Citation Counts | | | |
		1	2	3	Total
46	Lorsch, JW	202	108	96	203
47	Tsoukas, H	202	102	87	195.5
48	Reger, R	200	115	76	195.5
49	Wruck, KH	324	34	31	194.5
50	Blake, RR	125	120	117	181
51	Ford, JD	158	104	94	178
52	Sproull, LS	228	65	51	172
53	Bedeian, A	124	121	87	166
54	French, W	128	119	84	165.5
55	Adler, NJ	114	104	93	155.5
56	Greiner, L	124	93	92	154.5
57	Barr, PS	121	107	80	154
58	Armenakis, AA	217	48	41	153
59	Beckhard, R	117	95	91	151.5
60	Stimpert, JL	117	107	65	144.5
61	Mauborgne, R	208	44	33	142.5
62	Cummings, TG	115	73	71	129.5
63	Mirvis, P	99	75	74	124
64	Golembiewski, RT	107	82	54	121.5
65	Hersey, P	117	60	60	118.5
66	Coch, L	103	68	63	117
67	Sashkin, M	84	78	64	113
68	Langley, A	86	76	60	111
69	Ledford, GE	130	49	40	109.5
70	Hirschhorn, L	80	69	66	107.5
71	Woodman, R	84	63	63	105
72	Beer, S	90	74	46	105
73	Burke, WW	73	58	57	94
74	Harrison, Roger	74	65	43	91
75	Stacey, RD	71	67	41	89.5
76	Rajagopalan, N	75	55	45	87.5
77	Brown, LD	67	58	49	87
78	Porras, JI	61	59	49	84.5
79	Davis, DA	62	56	48	83
80	Potter, J	68	47	40	77.5
81	Heneman, RL	97	29	24	75
82	Miller, RH	94	20	18	66
83	Dunphy, D	46	44	42	66
84	Moore, L	44	43	39	63
85	Tannenbaum, R	36	34	34	52
86	Pasmore, WA	39	32	31	51
87	Cooperrider, D	42	29	29	50
88	Palmer, I	44	34	20	49
89	White, MC	38	20	19	38.5
90	Cohen, AR	27	26	21	37

Table 6 (Cont.)

Rank Order of Average Largest Co-citation Intersections (Cont.)

Rank	Author	Largest Citation Counts			Total
		1	2	3	
91	Goodstein, LD	27	26	19	36
92	Benne, KD	30	21	21	36
93	Hornstein, H	34	18	18	35
94	French, JL	23	23	21	33.5
95	Stevenson, WB	23	22	20	32.5
96	Mouton, JS	41	11	9	30.5
97	Bushe, G	25	20	16	30.5
98	Prasad, P	21	19	19	29.5
99	Sebastian, JG	47	6	5	29
100	Schaffer, RH	21	17	15	26.5
101	Huy, QN	16	15	15	23
102	Kakabadse, A	15	15	14	22
103	Stewart, WH	10	10	10	15
104	Mathews, J	11	7	7	12.5
105	van Dick, R	12	6	5	11.5
106	Shani, R	6	5	4	7.5
107	Eddy, W	6	5	4	7.5
108	Quinn, RW	3	2	2	3.5
109	Hough, JR	3	2	2	3.5
110	Greve, MS	4	2	1	3.5
111	Harris, RT	2	2	1	2.5

Also to ensure that the ranking being returned by the co-citation counts was feasible, the 20 authors with the largest diagonals were compared against the list of the top 20 authors with the highest sole citation counts. Of those 20 authors, 16 fell in the top 20 on both lists, confirming that those authors with high co-citation diagonals were heavily cited.

As the co-citation counts were a better representation of impact to the field, those counts were used to determine those authors that had significantly impacted the field of change management. But further analysis was needed to accurately portray the authors' exact impact. For example the top three authors with the largest diagonals were Prochaska, DiClemente, and Bandura; while it was evident that they had significantly contributed to the field of change management, it is hard to gauge the extent of their impact. Prochaska's three largest co-citation intersections with other authors were 3,976 (intersecting with DiClemente), 1,620 (intersecting with Bandura), and 58 (intersecting with Lewin), while DiClemente's were 3,976 (intersecting with Prochaska), 1,336 (intersecting with Bandura), and 43 (intersecting with Moore), and finally Bandura's largest co-citation intersections were 1,620 (intersecting with Prochaska), 1,336 (intersecting with DiClemente) and 611 (intersecting with Lewin). These three authors had repeatedly cited with each other, but in the case of Prochaska and DiClemente whose third highest intersections were 58 and 43, it was apparent that they had relative few co-citations with other authors outside of the top threesome. This suggests that Prochaska and DiClemente's work may not be integrated completely into much of the mainstream change literature. This drove further analysis to assess the relation of each of these significant authors within the field of change management.

Phase III – Statistical Analysis

To answer the second research question regarding what specific subgroups have evolved within the field of change management, along with determining what relationships existed between individual authors, a factor analysis was conducted on the co-citation matrix developed during Phase II. The co-citation counts within the matrix varied from a high of 3,976 to many author intersections with a count of 1 or 0. In order to conduct a factor analysis on the co-citation data the counts contained in the matrix was normalized such that the results would not be skewed due to these differences in magnitude. Consistent with White (2003), the raw co-citation matrix was used to compute correlations (using MS Excel) and are presented in Appendix C. To ensure the best possible representation of the data found in the co-citation matrix, the diagonal for each author was used in place of the author's co-citation with himself or herself (White, 2003). The correlation matrix was then used as a basis for conducting a factor analysis in *SPSS*. The factor analysis was conducted such that all factors with an eigenvalue greater than one were retained. Also, consistent with the method set forth by Culnan (1986) and White and Griffith (1981), factor loadings less than 0.4 were suppressed. Finally, a varimax rotation was used to help find the best fit.

Twelve factors emerged from the first analysis (i.e., those with eigenvalues greater than 1). Those 12 factors accounted for 93.24 percent of the variation (see Appendix D), with all of the authors loading onto one of the factors. However, upon further review several of the factors returned only included two or three authors that were also cross loaded with other factors. Consistent with Tabachnick and Fidell (1983) those factors with few author loadings were studied to determine whether they should be included as separate factors. This was done by observing the correlation data associated with each of the authors. If the authors in question were highly correlated only with each other, then they might constitute a separate factor. However, if the authors in question were not exclusively correlated with each other, then the factor in question might be unreliable. After removing those factors that were problematic, the data was factor analyzed again, limiting the results to the ideal number of factors. This second factor analysis was done while still retaining all authors included in the study,

Six factors were determined to best represent the data. These six factors accounted for 84.49 percent of the variation (see Appendix E). Of the six factors; 110 authors loaded on at least one factor, 20 authors loaded onto two factors, one author loaded onto three factors, and one author failed to load onto any factor. The majority of the authors loaded onto the first two factors, each of them being of the approximate same size of 50 authors, while the remaining four factors each contained between six and four authors. To which factor each author was loaded is displayed in Table 7, while the complete factor analysis and factor loadings are found in Appendix F.

Once the author loadings on the six factors were determined, further searches were conducted using the *SSCI* database to identify papers that were: written by the authors loaded to each factor and those papers that co-cite authors on each factor. This was done such that common themes could be identified in each factor, allowing for factor names to be given.

By naming factors one and two first, it was possible to more easily identify common themes within the rest of the factors, due to the close relationship between factors one and two with factors three, four and six. Due to the large number of authors which loaded to factors one and two it was unfeasible to study all of the papers written by the authors loaded to each factor, or those papers that co-cite two of the authors due to the large number of documents identified in the *SSCI*. To provide a reasonable group of documents from which to draw a common theme, a sample of authors in each factor was studied. In each of the two factors, the citation references for the papers written by the ten authors with the largest factor loadings to each factor where obtained for further study. These citation references contained a paper title and occasionally a paper abstract which were used as a basis for analysis. In addition, the citation references for the papers that co-cite the five authors with the largest factor loadings in each factor were collected to help in identifying a common theme for the factor.

Even when a sampling of authors was used as a basis of study there were large numbers of citations returned. For factor one, the number of author written citations returned was 566, for factor two it was 536 (because of the large number of authors included in both of these factors, only citations were obtained from the ten authors with the largest factor loading). The number of co-citations returned for factor one were 534 and for factor two 3,592 citations were returned. To identify a common theme, those citations from authors in each factor were skimmed and recurring ideas or subjects from each author were identified. This list of recurring ideas and subjects was then analyzed by looking for common themes or patterns among the different authors. Once one or more common themes were identified, that theme was then checked by conducting searches for key terms in connection with the identified theme among those citations which were obtained from the co-citation of the authors on the factor. This was done as authors were typically co-cited when they wrote on similar ideas.

Some of the recurring ideas found in factor one included: group, organization, planning, leadership, behavior, practice, and conflict. This is illustrated by some of the papers written by authors that were included in this factor; Bennis and Jamieson (1981) "Organization development at the crossroads," Burke, Richley, and Deangelis (1985) "Changing leadership and planning processes at the Lewis-Research-Center, National-Aeronautics-and-Space Administration," Feinberg, Ostroff, and Burke (2005) "The role of within-group agreement in understanding transformational leadership," Robertson, Roberts and Porras (1993) "Dynamics of planned organizational-change - Assessing empirical support for a theoretical-model," Schein, Beckhard, and Driscoll (1980)

"Teaching organizational-psychology to middle managers – a process approach," and Walton (1980) "Planned changes to improve organizational-effectiveness."

In factor two some of the ideas present were: strategy, theory, model, content, system, process, and stage. Some examples of papers from this factor include; Angle, Manz, and Van de Ven (1985) "Integrating human-resource management and corporate-strategy – A preview of the 3M story," Astley and Van de Ven (1983) "Central perspectives and debate in organization theory," Barr, Stimpert, and Huff (1992) "Cognitive change, strategic action, and organizational renewal," Huff (2000) "Changes in organizational knowledge production," Jarzabkowski (2003) "Strategic practices: An activity theory perspective on continuity and change," Labianca, Gray and Brass (2000) "A grounded model of organizational schema change during empowerment," Markus and Robey (1988) "Information technology and organizational-change – Causal-structure in theory and research,"

Upon examination of the ideas present, factor one contained authors that wrote at an organizational level, focusing on applying change to an organization. With this in mind, the name given to factor one is ORGANIZATION & GROUP DEVELOPMENT. While the analysis of the ideas present in factor two seemed to point to the fact that authors in that group tended to write more on change theory in general terms, including process and strategy; because of this, the factor was given the name CHANGE THEORY.

Once factors one and two had been named, it was possible to move on and identify common themes in factors three, four and six. Upon analysis of the factor loadings, factor three was determined to be related to factor one, and factors four and six

41

were related to factor two due to the level of cross-loading between the factors. With factors one and two named, it was possible to see how the authors in factors three, four and six differed in their research from those authors in factors one and two. The same method of analysis for both author citations and co-cited citations that was used on factors one and two was applied here. Other than due to the small number of authors loaded on factors three, four and six, all authors were analyzed and not just a sampling from the factor.

There were 256 citations found that had been written by the authors loaded onto factor three, in conjunction, there were 781 citations that co-cite at least two of the authors from the factor. Upon analysis of the authors' paper citations some recurring ideas included: psychological contracts, trust, performance, commitment, process, and preparedness. Some examples includes; Caldwell and Karri (2005) "Organizational governance and ethical systems: A covenantal approach to building trust," Meyer, Allen and Topolnytsky (1998) "Commitment in a changing world of work," Robinson, Kraatz, and Rousseau (1994) paper, "Changing obligations and the psychological contract – a longitudinal study," Rousseau (1998) "Why workers still identify with organizations," and Sparrowe and Liden (1997) "Process and structure in leader-member exchange," These ideas suggest that factor three authors write concerning the processes leading up to change or preparing for change. With these ideas the name chosen to identify factor three is CHANGE INITIATION/DIAGNOSIS.

Factors four and six were not only related to factor two but to each other. The number of author citations obtained was 188 for factor four and 119 for factor six. The number of citations obtained from author co-citations in each factor were: factor four –

581, and factor six – 1115. Further analysis of these factors found that both had the recurring theme of corporate management and change; while factor four focused on investments, acquisitions and finances and factor six authors tended toward corporate strategy as an overarching theme. With the similarities evident between the two factors, it was possible that they might be combined into just one factor. However, when a factor analysis was conducted on those authors found in factors four and six, forcing them into just one factor, only 49 percent of the variance was explained. It was decided that this amount of the variance explained was insufficient to justify combining the two factors into one (Spicer, 2005), suggesting that enough difference existed between the authors of the two factors and what they write on to validate separate factors. In the end, the factors where given the names; factor four – CORPORATE FINANCIAL CHANGE, and factor six – CORPORATE STRATEGIC CHANGE. These names were based on papers such as Anderson and Campbell (2004) "Corporate governance of Japanese banks," Denis (1990) "Defensive changes in corporate payout policy – share repurchases and special dividends," and Jensen (1993) "The modern industrial-revolution, exit, and the failure of internal control-systems" for factor four, and Bartlett and Ghoshal (1994) "Changing the role of top management – beyond strategy to purpose," Boter and Holmquist (1996) "Industry characteristics and internationalization processes in small firms," and finally McDougall and Oviatt (1996) "New venture internationalization, strategic change, and performance: A follow-up study" for factor six.

Finally, 242 citations were used to identify a possible common theme from the authors in factor five. Among the ideas present were: readiness, models, social cognition and overwhelmingly individual change. These ideas were cross-checked with 2,785 citations that cited at least two of the authors on the factor. The idea of individual change was consistently present throughout the citations, as evident by the following documents; Bandura (2004) "Health promotion by social cognitive means," Moore (1995) "Getting past the rapids – individuals and change," Prochaska, Diclemente, and Norcross (1992) "In search of how people change – Applications to addictive behaviors," and Snow, Prochaska, and Rossi (1994) "Processes of change in Alcoholics-Anonymous – Maintenance factors in long-term sobriety." With this in mind the name chosen to represent factor five is – INDIVIDUAL CHANGE.

As stated in the method, a multidimensional scaling analysis (MDS) was conducted on the correlation data to provide a pictorial representation of the field of change management. Once again a limitation in the *SPSS* software on the number of variables that can be analyzed prevented the inclusion of all 111 authors in the MDS. As only 100 authors could be included in the analysis, 11 authors had to be dropped from the pictorial representation. As the MDS provides a way to visually show the results obtained from the factor analysis, it was decided to remove the 11 authors with the smallest factorial loadings from the first two factors such that there would still be sufficient authors included in those factors to give shape to the region in which those factors inhabit. Removing authors from any of the smaller factors might compromise how they are pictorially displayed in the MDS. The resulting graph (Graph 1, shown below) shows how the various factors are interrelated to each other. Factors one and two are clearly defined, with factor 3 providing a bridge between those two. Factor five was unique and separated from the others. The remaining factors, four and six appear to be interrelated with factor two.

Table 7.

Author Factor Loadings

Factor 1		Factor 2		Factor 3	
Bennis, W	0.976	Daft, RL	0.955	Bedeian, A	0.757
Beer, M	0.956	Van de Ven, AH	0.953	Rousseau, D	0.706
Beckhard, R	0.953	Weick, KE	0.950	Morrison, EW	0.700
Harrison, Roger	0.951	Ford, JD	0.948	Heneman, RL	0.680
French, W	0.951	Tushman, M	0.939	van Dick, R	0.636
Coch, L	0.932	Langley, A	0.934	Armenakis, AA	0.580
Burke, WW	0.931	Gray, B	0.912		
Sashkin, M	0.930	Poole, MS	0.910		
Porras, JI	0.918	Huff, AS	0.902		
Walton, RE	0.917	Bower, JL	0.901	**Factor 4**	
Goodstein, LD	0.915	Greenwood, R	0.901	Wruck, KH	0.763
Golembiewski, RT	0.915	Pettigrew, AM	0.894	Lorsch, JW	0.718
Blake, RR	0.915	Tsoukas, H	0.884	Greve, MS	0.674
Pasmore, WA	0.909	Romanelli, E	0.879	Jensen, MC	0.624
Benne, KD	0.909	Galbraith, JR	0.876	Potter, J	-0.613
Dunphy, D	0.908	Lawrence, PR	0.875	Mathews, J	0.410
Kakabadse, A	0.907	Stewart, WH	0.852		
Schein, E	0.906	Reger, R	0.845		
Cummings, TG	0.903	Stacey, RD	0.823		
Tannenbaum, R	0.899	Nelson, RR	0.820	**Factor 5**	
Harris, RT	0.897	Kiesler, S	0.811	Bandura, A	-0.850
Bushe, G	0.888	Prasad, P	0.807	Davis, DA	-0.838
Lewin, K	0.881	Stevenson, WB	0.799	Moore, L	-0.838
Schaffer, RH	0.881	Barr, PS	0.792	Prochaska, JO	-0.795
Kotter, J	0.877	Bartunek, J	0.791	DiClemente, CC	-0.790
Argyris, C	0.869	Powell, WW	0.769	Miller, RH	-0.546
Hornstein, H	0.866	Rajagopalan, N	0.766		
Mirvis, P	0.866	Hough, JR	0.766		
Conger, JA	0.846	Boeker, W	0.756		
Lawler, EE	0.844	DiMaggio, P	0.747	**Factor 6**	
Hirschhorn, L	0.840	Zajac, EJ	0.744	Bartlett, CA	0.736
Eddy, W	0.836	Greiner, L	0.743	Kim, WC	0.732
Hersey, P	0.829	Shortell, SM	0.737	Mauborgne, R	0.712
Cooperrider, D	0.824	Stimpert, JL	0.733	Ghoshal, S	0.656
Woodman, R	0.798	French, JL	0.715	Adler, NJ	0.600
Cohen, AR	0.792	Nohria, N	0.714		
Senge, PM	0.772	Alvesson, M	0.705		
Ledford, GE	0.729	White, MC	0.705		
Kanter, RM	0.709	Palmer, I	0.689	**Did Not Load to a Factor**	
Brown, LD	0.693	Huy, QN	0.657	Sebastian, JG	
Beer, S	0.670	O'Reilly, C	0.650		
Shani, R	0.560	Quinn, RW	0.649		
Mouton, JS	0.515	Winter, SG	0.643		
		Sproull, LS	0.566		

Figure 3. MDS Map of Co-citation Data

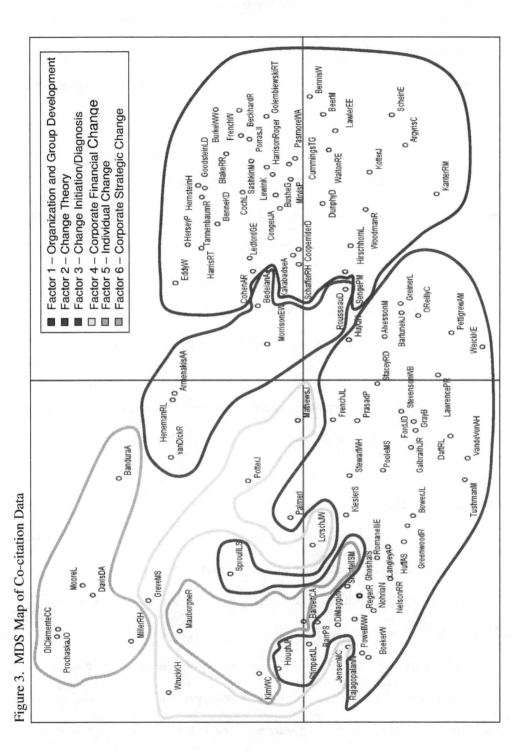

IV. Discussion

Organizations exist in a changing world where they must constantly adapt to survive. Researchers have consistently worked to provide better insight and knowledge to practitioners to help in successfully implementing organizational change. Several qualitative reviews of organizational change research have identified the specific investigative threads that have been pursued by those studying change. These reviews indicate that several aspects of change have been explored to include the processes that should be employed to bring about successful change, how other forces affect organizational change, and what outcomes can be expected as a result of change. In addition, researchers have crossed disciplinary boundaries, such as medical practitioners, educators, social scientists, as all types of organizations are interested in successful change.

While all of this research has provided insight into the nature of change, how far has the field matured toward a unifying theory? Kuhn (1962), in his discourse on the nature of scientific revolutions, suggests that a field of study matures as it converges toward a unified theory built upon the work of preceding research. While the study of organizational development and change has existed for some time, researchers within the field continue to make repeated calls for this convergence to occur (Armenakis & Bediean, 1999; Barnett & Carroll, 1995; Friedlander & Brown, 1974; Rajagopalan & Spreitzer, 1996; Woodman, 1989).

The nature of this research was to quantitatively observe and map the field of change management by using a co-citation methodology to determine where it stands in regards to cross discipline integration and theory convergence. It also determined the relative importance of individual authors' contributions to the field according to their number of co-citations with other change researchers. The culmination of this effort was a map of change research, showing the different sub-groups that exist within the field, along with what authors are associated with those groups. This map displays the level of integration existent within the field of change management and will provide future researchers a road map on what areas need to be further worked to provide the convergence of thought that so many researchers within the field are calling for.

The first question posed was what authors have significantly impacted the field of change management. As was discussed in the results, the co-citation counts obtained and their subsequent intersections were considered the best gauge of an author's significance to the field. By using co-citations, the chance of counting erroneous citations was minimized. The ranking that was obtained was interesting, however, in that while it provided insight into which authors had been repeated cited by other researchers, it might not have fully addressed actual importance to the field.

As was shown in the results, Prochaska, DiClemente, and Bandura had the highest co-citation count intersections. These authors were repeatedly co-cited with each other but had relatively low co-citation counts with other change researchers. Although there is little argument that that these three have made significant contributions to the field, the extent to which this influence has permeated through the study of all change may be limited to their area of specialty, namely, individual change. Their effect on the rest of the body of change management might be limited as evident by the low co-citation counts with authors that deal more with general organizational change. With this in mind, the results obtained are probably best used in determining level of contribution to the field, but their use as a gauge of actual importance should be limited without further research into their effect on the field.

From the list of authors, statistical techniques were applied to the co-citation counts to more clearly illuminate the sub-groups within the field. This provided insight into how research within change management is being grouped, along with which authors are contributing to each aspect of change research. This idea of identifying sub-groups within the field was also used to determine the level of integration across disciplines, and also theory convergence within the field. In the end, as shown in the result, change research appears to revolve around six areas. These included: Organization & Group Development, Change Theory, Change Initiation/Diagnosis, Corporate Financial Change, Corporate Strategic Change, and Individual Change. Largely, these focus areas were not discipline-specific such as medical change or change in educational institutions. Change researchers in all disciplines are building upon the work of each other in an effort to develop better theory and practices toward successful change. This suggests some level of integration lending some evidence that the call for integration made by Van de Ven and Poole (1995) has been heeded and continues to evolve.

Yet, while interdisciplinary integration is taking place, the idea of convergence within the field, and specifically that between content and process issues of change (Barnett & Carroll, 1995, Rajagopalan & Spreitzer, 1996) may not have occurred to a great extent. The two major groups that formed during the study, [Organization & Group Development (process)] and [Change Theory (content)], illustrate that most researchers within the field of change management still concentrate on one or the other aspects of change. When observed mathematically using a multidimensional scaling analysis, it was found that there is some limited bridging effort being done by the authors that were grouped together under the Change Initiation/Diagnosis factor. But even then, those researchers were primarily focused on the processual approach to change looking at ways to initiate change, and measure its progression (Armenakis & Harris, 2002; Bedeian & Feild, 2002; Day & Bedeian, 1991; Heneman, 1988; Jordan, Field, & Armenakis, 2002).

Also, convergence of research among all the groups is decidedly lacking when the aspect of individual change is taken into account. Researchers agree that individual change is vital to overall organizational change (Beer & Walton, 1987; Pasmore and Fagans, 1992), yet little work has been done to incorporate the work done by those researchers that concentrate specifically on individual change such as Prochaska and DiClemente into the overall theory of change.

However, the map of change research does provide insights into what areas of the field need further work and refinement. It highlights areas that have few contributing researchers and that might provide ground for new research. This further refinement and contribution to needed areas can lead to a better understand of change and possible further blending of theory.

Implications

For change researchers, this study provides a mathematical map to the nature of change management literature as defined by significant authors with field. Areas that need further work and refinement are highlighted along with where current researchers are working. Guidance as to what additional work needs to be done to help move the field toward a unifying theory on change can be gained by looking at what work has been done in the past towards convergence, where the different sub-groups currently stand, and what research gaps in the field need to be filled.

Also, change is a multi-level process that happens at the individual, group, and organizational level simultaneously. In addition, it is a process that unfolds over time. Thus, there is a need to conduct multi-level studies that examine the phenomenon over time. Understanding this is difficult to do within the context of a single study; researchers must take strides to capture this reality. By doing this, the field can continue to work towards convergence.

Limitations

One shortcoming to the study was that not all authors involved with change management could be studied and classified. Because the decision was made to use those authors considered influential by noted change researchers, some level of bias could have been introduced as those researchers could have given author names or publications where they themselves figured prominently. This could have been overcome by including all change authors, but due to the scope of that effort it was unfeasible. Also, the co-citation method used in obtaining the results, while useful in classifying and studying a group of authors, becomes difficult to manage with the size of the author group selected for study.

Another limitation of the method is that the results are only as good as the data obtained from the reference database. While the *Social Sciences Citation Index (SSCI)* is comprehensive in its coverage of change literature, it may not include all work done by change researchers such as that published in books and book series. Also, the narrowed scope of *SSCI* available for use in this study restricted the range of available documents.

While citation data prior to 1980 was available within the database, the database only looks at works cited from documents published since 1980. This meant that co-citation counts were unavailable on all papers published prior to 1980.

Also, citation counts also give more credence to older authors versus younger ones. The time lag in publishing a manuscript means that the likelihood increases that a significant, fledgling author who has recently appeared on the scene will not be captured for several years, and thus not be included in this study.

Future Research Opportunities

Further work needs to be done by actually studying what the sub-group's authors' individual papers provide to the field, especially with regards to those authors that have begun to make the transition between content and process aspects of the field. Looking at what work has been done by those authors will give future researchers working toward integration a better idea of what has been done and where the direction of their work should go.

Also, further work in the field needs to be done to integrate the work done by individual change researchers with the main body of change theory. A better understanding of the individual change process will help in understanding how both groups and organizations change (Burke, 2002).

Summary

In the end, there is still a lot of work that needs to be done in the field of change management. While it is important to understand what the field looks like today, more importantly it needs to be used as a basis for further research that can help move towards a unifying theory of change. For the field of change to reach the maturity spoken of by

Kuhn (1962), more work needs to be done to incorporate the different ideas and theories represented by the groups found in this study. As content theories are intermeshed with process theories, and with the incorporation of individual change ideas, a unifying theory of change can begin to emerge. This unifying theory will hopefully help organizations survive in today's evolving world, by providing them the tools to successfully adapt their organizations to meet new and emerging demands that will be placed on them. And hopefully all this change can be implemented with a better success than we now enjoy.

Authors of Organizational Change Papers

Academy of Management Review

"Conflicting uses of metaphors: Reconceptualizing their use in field of organizational change" (1999)

    Ian Palmer (University of Technology, Sydney, Australia)
    Ian.Palmer@uts.edu.au
    Richard Dunford (Victoria University of Wellington, New Zealand)
    Not Contacted

"Explaining development and change in organizations" (1995)

    Andrew H Van De Ven (University of Minnesota)
    avandeve@umn.edu
    Marshall Scott Poole (Texas A&M)
    mspoole@tamu.edu

"Organizational silence: A banner to change and development" (2000)

    Elizabeth Wolfe Morrison (NYU)
    emorriso@stern.nyu.edu
    Frances J Milliken (NYU)
    fmillike@stern.nyu.edu

"Role of conversations in producing intentional change in organizations" (1995)

    Jeffrey D Ford (The Ohio State University)
    ford.1@osu.edu
    Laurie W Ford (Critical Path Consulting)
    Not Contacted

"Time, temporal capability and planned change" (2001)

    Quy Nguyen Huy (Insead, Fontainebleau, France)
    quy.huy@insead.edu

"Toward a theory of strategic change: A multi-lens per. and integrative frame" (1997)

    Nandini Rajagopalan (University of Southern California)
    nrajagop@marshall.usc.edu
    Gretchen M Spreitzer (USC)
    Not Contacted

"Understanding radical organizational change: Bringing together old and new institutionalism" (1996)
> Royston Greenwood (University of Alberta, Edmonton)
> royston.greenwood@ualberta.ca
> C. R. Hinings (University of Alberta, Edmonton)
> Not Contacted

Annual Review of Psychology

"Organizational change and development" (1999)
> Karl E. Weick (University of Michigan)
> karlw@umich.edu
> Robert E. Quinn (University of Michigan)
> requinn@umich.edu

"Organizational innovation and organizational change" (1999)
> J. T. Hage (University of Maryland)
> hage@socy.umd.edu

Journal of Applied Psychology

"Commitment to organizational change: Extension of three component model" (2002)
> Lynne Herscovitch (University of Western Ontario)
> Not Contacted
> John P Meyer (University of Western Ontario)
> meyer@uwo.ca

"Resistance to change: Developing and individual differences measure" (2003)
> Shavl Oreg (Cornell)
> so44@cornell.edu

"The role of change in relationships between communication and turnover: A latent growth modeling approach" (2005)
> Kathleen Bentein (University of Quebec at Montreal)
> bentein.kathleen@uqam.ca
> Robert Vanderberg (University of Georgia)
> Not Contacted

"What's a good reason to change?" – (1999)
> Denise M Rousseau (Carnegie Mellon University)
> rousseau@andrew.cmu.edu
> Snehal A Tijoriwala (Carnegie Mellon University)
> Not Contacted

Journal of Management

"Convergence vs. strategic reorientation: antecedents of fast paced organizational change" (2000)

Shelly S Gordon (M.B. Associates)
Wayne H Stewart (Clemson)
waynes@clemson.edu
Robert Sweo (University of Maryland)
Not Contacted
William A Luker (University of North Texas)
Not Contacted

"Formal analysis of narratives of organizational change" (1998)

William B Stevenson (Boston College)
william.stevenson.1@bc.edu
Danna N. Greenberg (Boston College)
Not Contacted

"Organizational change: A review of theory & research in the 1990s" (1999)

Achilles A Armenakis (Auburn)
armenac@auburn.edu
Arthur G. Bedeian (Louisiana State University)
abede@lsu.edu

"Using stories to create change: The object lesson of Frederick Taylor's pig-tale" (2001)

Jill R Hough (University of Tulsa)
jill-hough@utulsa.edu
Margaret A White (Oklahoma State)
margaret.white@okstate.edu

Editors of Selected Journals on Organizational Change

Academy of Management Review

Editors:
Martin Kilduff (Pennsylvania State University)
mxk6@psu.edu

Ming-Jer Chen (University of Virginia)
ChenM@darden.virginia.edu

Thomas Donaldson (University of Pennsylvania)
donaldst@wharton.upenn.edu

Violina Rindova (University of Maryland)
vrindova@rhsmith.umd.edu

Loriann Roberson (Arizona State University)
loriann.roberson@asu.edu

Pamela Tolbert (Cornell University)
pst3@cornell.edu

Aks Zaheer (University of Minnesota)
zahee002@umn.edu

Ajay Mehra (University of Cincinnati)
ajaymehra1@gmail.com

Administrative Science Quarterly (ASQ)

Editor:
Donald A. Palmer (University of California-Davis)
dapalmer@ucdavis.edu

Associate Editors:
Daniel J. Brass (University of Kentucky)
dbrass@uky.edu

Hayagreeva Rao (Stanford University)
hrao@stanford.edu

Elaine Romanelli (Georgetown University)
romanele@georgetown.edu

John A. Wagner, III (Michigan State University)
wagner@msu.edu

Consulting Editors:
Mauro Guillén (University of Pennsylvania)
guillen@wharton.upenn.edu

Kathleen McGinn (Harvard University)
kmcginn@hbs.edu

Annual Review of Psychology

Editors:
Susan T. Fiske (Princeton University)
sfiske@Princeton.edu

Alan E. Kazdin (Yale University, School of Medicine)
alan.kazdin@yale.edu

Daniel L. Schacter (Harvard University)
dls@wjh.harvard.edu

Industrial and Corporate Change

Editors:
David Teece (University of California, Berkeley)
teece@haas.berkeley.edu

Paul Nightingale (University of Sussex, UK)
p.nightingale@sussex.ac.uk

Nick Von Tunzelmann (University of Sussex, UK)
g.n.von-tunzelmann@sussex.ac.uk

The Journal of Applied Behavioral Science

Editor:
Richard Woodman (Texas A&M)
r-woodman@tamu.edu

Journal of Applied Psychology

Editor:
Sheldon Zedeck (University of California-Berkeley)
zedeck@socrates.berkeley.edu

Journal of Change Management

Editor:
Colin Carnall (Warwick University, UK)
colin.carnall@wbs.ac.uk

Journal of Management

Editor:
Russell Cropanzano (University of Arizona)
russell@eller.arizona.edu

Journal of Organizational Change Management

Editor:
Slawomir Magala (Erasmus University Rotterdam, Netherlands)
jocm.magala@fbk.eur.nl

Regional Editors:
Hugo Letiche (University of Humanist Studies, Netherlands)
h.letiche@uvh.nl

Cliff Oswick (Kings College, The University of London, UK)
clifford.oswick@kcl.ac.uk

Adrian Carr (University of Western Sydney, Australia)
a.carr@uws.edu.au

David Boje (New Mexico State University)
dboje@nmsu.edu

Alexis Downs (Emporia State University)
downsale@emporia.edu

Journal of Strategic Change

Editors:
Graham Beaver (Nottingham Business School, UK)
graham.beaver@ntu.ac.uk

Chris Prince (Nottingham Business School, UK)
christopher.prince@ntu.ac.uk

Leadership & Organization Development Journal

Editor:
Marie McHugh (University of Ulster, UK)
ml.mchugh@ulster.ac.uk

Associate Editor:
Andrew Kakabadse (Cranfield School of Management, UK)
a.p.kakabadse@cranfield.ac.uk

Research in Organizational Change and Development

Editor:
Richard Woodman (Texas A&M)
r-woodman@tamu.edu

Additional Suggested Scholars

Kim Boal (Texas Tech University)
kim.boal@ttu.edu

John Ivancevich (University of Houston)
jivance@uh.edu

Alan Glassman (Cal State Northridge)
aglassman@csun.edu

Tom Cumming (USC)
tcummings@marshall.usc.edu

Mary Jo Hatch (University of Virginia)
mjh9d@virginia.edu

Linda Putnam (Texas A&M)
lputnam@tamu.edu

Barbara Gray (Pennsylvania State University)
b9g@psu.edu

Jean Bartunek (Boston College)
jean.bartunek.1@bc.edu

Researchers from the Medical and Educational Fields

Marshall Sashkin (George Washington University)
sashkin@gwu.edu

Julie G. Sebastian (University of Kentucky)
jgseba00@uky.edu

Robert H. Miller (University of California-San Francisco)
Robert.Miller@ucsf.edu

Liane R. Ginsburg (York University, UK)
lgins@yorku.ca

Deborah Tregunno (York University, UK)
tregunno@yorku.ca

Appendix B

Co-citation Counts

	Adler, NJ	Alvesson, M	Argyris, C	Armenakis, AA	Bandura, A	Barr, PS	Bartlett, CA	Bartunek, J	Beckhard, R	Bedeian, A	Beer, M	Beer, S	Benne, KD	Bennis, W	Blake, RR	Boeker, W	Bower, JL	Brown, LD	Burke, WW	Bushe, G	Coch, L	Cohen, AR
Adler, NJ	–	17	26	4	51	2	114	9	3	17	19	1	0	14	16	6	3	2	4	2	0	2
Alvesson, M	17	–	111	7	21	2	17	38	4	10	19	10	0	22	6	1	12	9	6	1	4	1
Argyris, C	26	111	–	26	199	42	65	157	91	47	157	90	17	290	120	28	77	58	58	14	68	11
Armenakis, AA	4	7	26	–	34	3	3	19	11	217	27	0	0	17	5	2	3	2	18	2	17	1
Bandura, A	51	21	199	34	–	7	21	39	11	80	38	2	5	83	45	19	16	9	12	3	26	27
Barr, PS	2	2	42	3	7	–	9	18	0	3	8	0	0	1	21	13	13	0	2	1	2	1
Bartlett, CA	114	17	65	3	21	9	–	15	6	8	26	8	0	22	2	13	63	0	1	2	0	0
Bartunek, J	9	38	157	19	39	18	15	–	17	16	31	7	3	35	21	15	15	19	10	5	11	4
Beckhard, R	3	4	91	11	11	0	6	17	–	10	61	8	9	95	42	4	4	9	30	7	13	2
Bedeian, A	17	10	47	217	80	3	8	16	10	–	20	2	2	23	7	11	11	2	16	6	5	2
Beer, M	19	19	157	27	38	8	26	31	61	20	–	3	2	70	34	6	7	9	51	7	22	3
Beer, S	1	10	90	0	2	0	8	7	8	2	3	–	0	13	5	1	7	6	0	1	2	0
Benne, KD	0	0	17	0	5	0	0	3	9	2	3	0	–	21	20	0	1	5	2	0	2	0
Bennis, W	14	22	290	17	83	1	22	35	95	23	70	13	21	–	84	8	13	15	51	10	30	13
Blake, RR	16	6	120	5	45	21	2	21	42	7	34	5	20	84	–	3	4	39	25	19	19	0
Boeker, W	6	1	28	2	19	13	13	15	4	11	6	1	0	8	3	–	19	5	0	1	0	2
Bower, JL	3	12	77	3	16	0	63	15	4	11	7	7	1	13	4	19	–	3	3	3	4	0
Brown, LD	2	9	58	2	9	0	0	19	9	2	9	6	5	15	39	5	3	–	6	7	3	1
Burke, WW	4	6	58	18	12	2	1	10	30	16	51	0	2	51	25	0	3	6	–	7	15	0
Bushe, G	2	1	14	2	3	1	2	5	7	6	7	1	0	10	19	1	3	7	7	–	4	0
Coch, L	0	4	68	17	26	2	0	11	13	5	22	2	2	30	19	0	4	3	15	4	–	0
Cohen, AR	2	1	11	1	27	1	0	4	2	2	3	0	0	13	0	2	0	1	0	0	0	–
Conger, JA	25	26	70	10	141	3	15	26	7	18	15	1	2	151	25	13	4	3	12	4	8	9
Cooperrider, D	4	13	42	2	4	3	5	16	5	0	9	2	0	13	1	1	1	15	5	9	4	1

Co-citation Counts

	Adler, NJ	Alvesson, M	Argyris, C	Armenakis, AA	Bandura, A	Barr, PS	Bartlett, CA	Bartunek, J	Beckhard, R	Bedeian, A	Beer, M	Beer, S	Benne, KD	Bennis, W	Blake, RR	Boeker, W	Bower, JL	Brown, LD	Burke, WW	Bushe, G	Coch, L	Cohen, AR
Cummings, TG	8	7	73	10	30	1	1	20	20	13	39	4	1	24	15	2	4	8	18	5	15	1
Daft, RL	41	50	328	11	111	48	94	130	9	49	35	21	3	65	16	42	89	13	7	6	13	1
Davis, DA	0	0	9	0	62	0	0	0	3	0	2	0	0	1	1	0	0	1	1	0	0	0
DiClemente, CC	0	0	7	3	1336	1	0	1	1	0	2	0	0	0	1	0	0	1	2	1	1	1
DiMaggio, P	46	68	145	4	71	29	95	53	9	14	31	11	1	30	4	116	52	25	4	1	3	0
Dunphy, D	16	10	39	8	18	3	9	13	9	5	33	2	4	41	2	6	2	2	7	2	6	1
Eddy, W	0	0	4	0	3	0	0	1	2	0	3	0	0	5	2	0	1	0	2	0	0	0
Ford, JD	5	32	65	9	44	20	12	35	8	17	24	5	1	16	1	16	14	4	2	0	7	3
French, JL	0	1	6	0	8	0	0	1	0	0	1	1	0	2	0	1	3	0	1	2	0	0
French, W	7	13	128	6	25	1	5	13	63	8	83	5	12	84	46	0	4	14	57	8	16	6
Galbraith, JR	30	15	139	4	36	6	106	26	18	15	37	26	4	48	12	25	90	15	9	3	6	3
Ghoshal, S	81	41	128	2	38	15	597	25	8	16	21	5	0	25	6	29	72	5	4	2	1	0
Golembiewski, RT	5	7	107	48	45	2	2	32	28	49	39	7	8	52	31	2	5	13	29	3	13	9
Goodstein, LD	6	4	17	1	9	0	2	2	9	3	7	0	2	19	9	0	2	0	26	1	0	1
Gray, B	27	30	78	4	24	13	27	58	3	8	15	4	3	28	15	14	16	67	9	2	4	0
Greenwood, R	8	47	81	7	46	21	16	78	8	9	23	17	2	27	8	25	27	4	7	2	2	0
Greiner, L	1	13	93	7	10	5	13	27	32	11	25	9	3	53	19	28	17	5	16	2	14	3
Greve, MS	0	0	0	0	0	0	0	0	0	0	0	0	0	1	0	0	0	0	0	0	0	0
Harris, RT	0	0	2	0	1	0	0	0	1	0	0	0	0	1	0	0	0	0	0	0	1	0
Harrison, Roger	4	13	65	6	21	0	2	7	21	8	26	9	3	43	22	0	0	3	12	3	5	3
Heneman, RL	2	0	7	2	10	0	0	2	2	29	13	0	0	4	1	2	2	0	4	2	1	0
Hersey, P	6	8	60	4	29	2	2	8	5	10	8	2	4	60	117	1	3	3	6	0	5	0
Hirschhorn, L	3	15	80	1	13	2	11	8	5	2	7	6	1	32	4	0	4	4	1	1	1	2
Hornstein, H	2	1	18	1	34	0	2	3	8	1	7	0	2	17	15	0	0	2	8	1	4	2

Co-citation Counts

	Adler, NJ	Alvesson, M	Argyris, C	Armenakis, AA	Bandura, A	Barr, PS	Bartlett, CA	Bartunek, J	Beckhard, R	Bedeian, A	Beer, M	Beer, S	Benne, KD	Bennis, W	Blake, RR	Boeker, W	Bower, JL	Brown, LD	Burke, WW	Bushe, G	Coch, L	Cohen, AR
Hough, JR	0	0	0	0	0	0	0	0	0	0	0	0	0	0	0	0	1	0	0	0	0	0
Huff, AS	7	22	114	9	21	121	28	60	4	11	15	7	0	8	4	43	49	1	2	1	6	1
Huy, QN	0	4	8	6	8	3	2	13	2	3	8	0	0	2	0	0	2	1	1	0	1	1
Jensen, MC	21	6	67	1	45	12	68	12	4	10	21	6	0	8	9	134	61	46	0	3	2	0
Kakabadse, A	1	2	15	1	2	0	0	6	3	1	7	1	1	0	2	1	1	2	2	0	1	1
Kanter, RM	104	110	387	35	212	14	101	51	39	85	120	23	6	234	64	37	79	27	40	16	34	26
Kiesler, S	12	6	100	4	115	22	15	33	0	6	5	5	2	20	13	18	18	4	1	3	5	2
Kim, WC	26	4	27	3	13	3	97	4	4	2	6	2	0	7	3	15	18	3	0	1	0	1
Kotter, J	29	46	188	41	71	7	48	43	39	32	108	13	3	196	32	28	36	7	39	5	31	16
Langley, A	4	15	22	1	7	8	9	18	3	2	9	2	0	3	0	11	26	2	3	1	1	0
Lawler, EE	29	27	286	20	237	2	22	20	31	87	134	14	5	98	41	4	19	11	40	25	63	12
Lawrence, PR	46	25	294	15	43	8	99	38	34	37	41	30	6	102	105	46	95	27	21	11	29	10
Ledford, GE	11	7	37	3	40	0	1	15	7	6	18	1	3	14	3	5	1	4	5	9	9	0
Lewin, K	28	43	389	38	611	8	16	56	60	46	75	29	30	171	92	8	11	49	46	7	103	12
Lorsch, JW	7	4	45	2	8	9	15	11	10	2	10	1	1	25	8	71	28	2	5	0	7	2
Mathews, J	0	1	7	0	6	0	2	0	0	1	4	2	0	1	0	0	0	1	1	0	0	0
Mauborgne, R	0	3	19	23	9	1	30	3	3	2	5	1	0	5	2	5	9	2	0	1	0	0
Miller, RH	0	0	7	1	18	0	0	0	0	1	1	0	5	2	1	2	0	20	1	0	0	0
Mirvis, P	11	9	58	9	29	1	6	16	13	20	27	2	0	21	20	0	2	6	17	7	11	3
Moore, L	4	2	0	1	39	0	1	0	1	1	0	5	0	0	0	0	0	3	0	0	0	1
Morrison, EW	9	15	71	6	98	3	14	14	2	33	14	4	0	10	3	6	6	6	0	0	3	3
Mouton, JS	3	1	7	0	5	0	1	1	1	0	0	0	0	4	41	0	1	0	0	0	1	1
Nelson, RR	15	30	239	4	111	22	92	26	4	9	18	18	0	15	3	81	133	8	2	1	8	2
Nohria, N	37	26	80	1	15	4	231	7	2	4	37	4	0	12	2	33	35	5	6	2	4	0

63

Appendix B (Cont.)

Co-citation Counts

	Adler, NJ	Alvesson, M	Argyris, C	Armenakis, AA	Bandura, A	Barr, PS	Bartlett, CA	Bartunek, J	Beckhard, R	Bedeian, A	Beer, M	Beer, S	Benne, KD	Bennis, W	Blake, RR	Boeker, W	Bower, JL	Brown, LD	Burke, WW	Bushe, G	Coch, L	Cohen, AR
O'Reilly, C	75	23	117	34	248	14	59	44	8	124	51	4	7	52	28	116	44	20	9	6	8	21
Palmer, I	0	44	12	3	2	1	3	5	0	1	3	0	0	3	2	3	1	3	2	0	0	1
Pasmore, WA	4	10	32	9	14	1	1	13	7	6	16	4	1	12	7	0	1	12	13	6	10	2
Pettigrew, AM	13	119	232	18	30	22	47	84	28	21	71	21	3	86	19	58	97	10	18	4	8	3
Poole, MS	25	31	86	13	40	15	14	33	7	15	18	4	11	32	17	11	12	5	4	1	4	1
Porras, JI	4	3	61	28	32	4	5	25	30	15	59	1	2	32	17	0	0	7	42	5	12	4
Potter, J	5	68	17	1	40	0	6	9	0	1	5	1	0	5	0	0	0	3	0	0	3	1
Powell, WW	54	81	186	4	64	29	130	55	9	13	34	12	0	37	7	129	72	24	3	2	4	1
Prasad, P	1	19	15	0	2	0	2	5	0	0	0	0	0	3	0	0	0	3	0	1	0	1
Prochaska, JO	0	0	11	5	1620	1	0	1	1	1	3	0	0	3	2	0	0	1	2	0	1	1
Quinn, RW	0	0	0	1	1	1	0	0	0	0	0	0	0	0	0	0	0	0	0	0	0	0
Rajagopalan, N	1	2	12	0	7	8	12	6	2	4	4	2	0	1	0	39	13	1	0	5	0	0
Reger, R	4	8	36	5	15	29	18	24	2	8	12	1	0	8	0	27	23	1	2	0	1	1
Romanelli, E	6	8	58	3	13	15	20	34	11	7	19	4	0	19	3	102	33	2	0	0	4	2
Rousseau, D	41	45	159	32	168	3	32	31	6	121	32	4	1	47	25	14	8	7	11	6	10	5
Sashkin, M	11	6	55	7	33	0	5	7	15	10	27	0	0	78	27	0	4	2	39	6	19	0
Schaffer, RH	0	2	17	0	5	0	2	0	3	1	21	1	0	5	0	1	1	0	3	2	1	0
Schein, E	93	164	773	39	213	20	71	112	117	78	159	38	21	306	106	35	45	23	73	20	49	9
Sebastian, JG	0	0	1	0	0	0	0	0	0	1	0	0	0	0	0	1	0	0	0	0	0	0
Senge, PM	11	29	486	12	63	15	35	32	17	12	64	46	3	59	11	9	23	7	23	5	5	2
Shani, R	1	0	3	0	0	0	0	1	1	0	2	0	0	1	0	0	0	0	0	3	0	0
Shortell, SM	2	14	45	7	35	15	16	11	2	7	17	0	1	15	6	56	20	36	4	2	2	0
Sproull, LS	0	7	26	4	10	3	4	14	1	5	1	0	1	5	3	0	5	2	0	1	2	1
Stacey, RD	1	15	67	2	1	6	6	4	3	4	12	12	0	8	0	5	5	0	3	1	1	0

Appendix B (Cont.)

Co-citation Counts

	Adler, NJ	Alvesson, M	Argyris, C	Armenakis, AA	Bandura, A	Barr, PS	Bartlett, CA	Bartunek, J	Beckhard, R	Bedeian, A	Beer, M	Beer, S	Benne, KD	Bennis, W	Blake, RR	Boeker, W	Bower, JL	Brown, LD	Burke, WW	Bushe, G	Coch, L	Cohen, AR
Stevenson, WB	8	5	5	1	6	0	5	5	0	4	4	0	0	6	3	5	1	0	0	1	2	2
Stewart, WH	1	0	4	0	10	0	1	0	0	0	1	4	0	2	1	2	2	1	0	0	0	0
Stimpert, JL	2	2	36	4	56	107	14	12	1	5	6	0	0	1	1	29	11	0	0	1	2	1
Tannenbaum, R	5	4	36	2	12	0	2	5	9	2	8	0	2	26	34	0	4	0	7	0	9	1
Tsoukas, H	5	102	87	4	8	4	11	31	3	8	11	32	0	10	2	5	6	1	3	2	0	2
Tushman, M	27	26	286	16	73	47	117	91	22	28	62	15	4	76	16	175	220	15	16	8	21	8
Van de Ven, AH	44	64	263	24	76	42	105	71	14	44	36	20	9	57	20	70	93	23	10	6	10	1
van Dick, R	0	0	1	0	5	1	0	0	1	0	0	0	0	0	1	0	0	0	1	1	0	0
Walton, RE	25	9	144	9	58	80	16	34	41	11	79	6	10	76	125	5	13	39	31	11	16	8
Weick, KE	57	231	644	34	252	4	116	207	33	68	93	74	8	160	42	76	148	29	17	11	24	11
White, MC	1	1	6	2	15	4	0	2	1	9	2	0	0	6	2	8	4	0	0	0	0	0
Winter, SG	3	13	98	0	9	5	52	7	0	4	5	5	0	2	1	26	52	1	0	0	0	0
Woodman, R	5	7	59	20	48	5	10	24	12	21	46	0	1	29	12	6	10	8	25	8	9	1
Wruck, KH	0	0	5	0	3	2	2	0	0	0	2	1	0	2	0	24	4	0	0	0	0	0
Zajac, EJ	16	9	46	3	31	32	43	19	2	7	7	1	1	3	3	179	41	9	1	0	2	3

Appendix B (Cont.)

Co-citation Counts

	Conger, JA	Cooprider, D	Cummings, TG	Daft, RL	Davis, DA	DiClemente, CC	DiMaggio, P	Dunphy, D	Eddy, W	Ford, JD	French, JL	French, W	Galbraith, JR	Ghoshal, S	Golembiewski, RT	Goodstein, LD	Gray, B	Greenwood, R	Greiner, L	Greve, MS	Harris, RT	Harrison, Roger	Heneman, RL
Adler, NJ	25	4	8	41	0	0	46	16	0	5	0	7	30	81	5	6	27	8	1	0	0	4	2
Alvesson, M	26	13	7	50	0	0	68	10	0	32	1	13	15	41	7	4	30	47	13	0	0	13	0
Argyris, C	70	42	73	328	9	7	145	39	4	65	6	128	139	128	107	17	78	81	93	0	2	65	7
Armenakis, AA	10	2	10	11	0	3	4	8	0	9	0	6	4	2	48	1	4	7	7	0	0	6	2
Bandura, A	141	4	30	111	62	1336	71	18	3	44	8	25	36	38	45	9	24	46	10	0	1	21	10
Barr, PS	3	3	1	48	0	1	29	3	0	20	0	1	6	15	2	0	13	21	5	0	0	0	0
Bartlett, CA	15	5	1	94	0	0	95	9	0	12	0	5	106	597	2	2	27	16	13	0	0	2	0
Bartunek, J	26	16	20	130	0	1	53	13	1	35	1	13	26	25	32	2	58	78	27	0	0	7	2
Beckhard, R	7	5	20	9	3	1	9	9	2	8	0	63	18	8	28	9	3	8	32	0	1	21	2
Bedeian, A	18	0	13	49	0	0	14	5	0	17	1	8	15	16	49	3	8	9	11	0	0	8	29
Beer, M	15	9	39	35	2	2	31	33	3	24	1	83	37	21	39	7	15	23	25	0	0	26	13
Beer, S	1	2	4	21	0	0	11	2	0	5	1	5	26	5	7	0	4	17	9	0	0	9	0
Benne, KD	2	0	1	3	0	0	1	4	0	1	0	12	4	0	8	2	3	2	3	0	0	3	0
Bennis, W	151	13	24	65	1	0	30	41	5	16	2	84	48	25	52	19	28	27	53	1	1	43	4
Blake, RR	25	1	15	16	1	1	4	2	2	1	0	46	12	6	31	9	15	8	19	0	0	22	1
Boeker, W	13	1	2	42	0	0	116	6	0	16	1	0	25	29	2	0	14	25	28	0	0	0	2
Bower, JL	4	1	4	89	0	0	52	2	1	14	3	4	90	72	5	2	16	27	17	0	0	0	2
Brown, LD	3	15	8	13	1	1	25	2	0	4	0	14	15	5	13	0	67	4	5	0	0	3	0
Burke, WW	12	5	18	7	1	2	4	7	2	2	0	57	9	4	29	26	9	7	16	0	0	12	4
Bushe, G	4	9	5	6	0	1	1	2	0	2	2	8	3	2	3	1	2	2	2	0	0	3	2
Coch, L	8	4	15	13	0	1	3	6	0	7	0	16	6	1	13	0	4	2	14	0	1	3	1
Cohen, AR	9	1	1	1	0	1	0	1	0	3	0	6	3	0	9	1	0	0	3	1	0	5	0
Conger, JA	-	4	12	31	0	0	20	9	0	5	1	5	16	20	16	0	16	15	8	0	0	11	2
Cooperrider, D	4	-	6	4	0	1	7	3	0	8	1	6	3	5	6	1	18	3	5	0	0	3	0

Co-citation Counts

	Heneman, RL	Harrison, Roger	Harris, RT	Greve, MS	Greiner, L	Greenwood, R	Gray, B	Goodstein, LD	Golembiewski, RT	Ghoshal, S	Galbraith, JR	French, W	French, JL	Ford, JD	Eddy, W	Dunphy, D	DiMaggio, P	DiClemente, CC	Davis, DA	Daft, RL	Cummings, TG	Cooperrider, D	Conger, JA
Cummings, TG	1	2	1	0	8	5	13	5	22	5	23	42	4	11	2	19	9	1	0	26	-	6	12
Daft, RL	5	3	0	0	37	90	84	2	16	159	354	16	21	94	1	10	203	1	1	-	26	4	31
Davis, DA	0	1	0	0	1	8	1	0	2	0	0	8	1	5	0	0	5	37	-	1	0	0	0
DiClemente, CC	0	2	0	0	3	7	0	2	7	0	0	1	1	0	0	2	0	-	37	1	1	1	0
DiMaggio, P	4	4	0	0	31	251	102	2	7	146	97	10	3	41	0	9	-	0	5	203	9	7	20
Dunphy, D	2	3	0	0	8	18	2	1	10	8	8	12	0	8	0	-	9	2	0	10	19	3	9
Eddy, W	0	0	0	0	2	1	0	1	6	0	8	2	2	0	-	8	0	2	0	1	2	0	0
Ford, JD	1	1	0	0	17	38	32	0	7	19	31	4	0	-	0	8	41	5	0	94	11	8	5
French, JL	3	2	0	0	3	2	3	1	7	4	6	0	-	2	0	0	3	1	8	21	4	1	1
French, W	4	33	0	0	23	4	10	14	35	7	16	-	0	4	2	12	10	1	8	16	42	6	5
Galbraith, JR	2	5	0	0	46	40	33	2	9	108	-	16	6	31	0	8	97	2	0	354	23	3	16
Ghoshal, S	2	3	0	0	15	49	48	1	4	-	108	7	4	19	0	8	146	0	0	159	5	5	20
Golembiewski, RT	5	14	1	0	17	6	12	8	-	4	9	35	1	7	6	10	7	2	0	16	22	6	16
Goodstein, LD	0	4	0	0	7	0	1	-	8	1	2	14	0	0	1	1	2	0	0	2	5	1	0
Gray, B	1	6	0	0	22	52	-	1	12	48	33	10	3	32	0	2	102	0	1	84	13	18	16
Greenwood, R	0	6	0	0	23	-	52	0	6	49	40	4	2	38	1	18	251	7	8	90	5	3	15
Greiner, L	2	14	0	0	-	23	22	7	17	15	46	23	3	17	2	8	31	3	1	37	8	5	8
Greve, MS	0	0	0	-	0	0	0	0	0	0	0	0	0	0	0	0	0	0	1	0	0	0	0
Harris, RT	0	0	-	0	0	0	0	0	1	0	0	0	0	0	0	0	0	0	0	0	1	0	0
Harrison, Roger	1	-	0	0	14	6	6	4	14	3	5	33	2	1	0	3	4	2	1	3	2	3	11
Heneman, RL	-	1	1	0	2	0	1	0	5	2	2	4	3	0	0	2	4	0	0	5	1	0	2
Hersey, P	1	5	0	0	10	4	2	3	6	4	7	8	0	2	0	6	3	2	0	8	3	0	44
Hirschhorn, L	1	4	0	0	1	5	8	1	8	5	15	2	1	10	1	6	10	1	1	22	10	3	8
Hornstein, H	1	6	0	0	4	0	3	4	7	2	1	10	0	1	0	1	0	0	0	2	4	1	5

Co-citation Counts

	Conger, JA	Cooperrider, D	Cummings, TG	Daft, RL	Davis, DA	DiClemente, CC	DiMaggio, P	Dunphy, D	Eddy, W	Ford, JD	French, JL	French, W	Galbraith, JR	Ghoshal, S	Golembiewski, RT	Goodstein, LD	Gray, B	Greenwood, R	Greiner, L	Greve, MS	Harris, RT	Harrison, Roger	Heneman, RL
Hough, JR	0	0	0	3	0	0	1	0	0	0	0	0	1	0	0	0	0	0	0	0	0	0	0
Huff, AS	9	7	2	128	0	1	92	7	0	51	0	5	27	45	6	0	31	56	17	0	0	3	2
Huy, QN	4	2	1	3	0	0	4	3	0	9	0	1	1	5	0	0	2	8	2	0	0	1	0
Jensen, MC	14	1	4	77	3	0	195	6	0	14	7	2	84	126	2	0	28	51	24	4	0	3	10
Kakabadse, A	2	2	0	2	0	0	2	1	0	0	0	8	2	2	3	0	4	0	7	0	0	6	0
Kanter, RM	129	12	59	207	2	4	217	44	0	38	23	39	171	124	41	13	103	67	74	0	1	32	11
Kiesler, S	7	1	6	375	0	2	69	2	1	29	4	2	54	46	7	2	20	25	15	0	0	1	3
Kim, WC	5	2	3	16	0	0	33	3	0	4	0	0	20	116	1	1	30	11	4	0	0	0	0
Kotter, J	108	7	32	88	3	5	52	32	0	31	5	45	70	62	19	7	29	41	45	2	0	10	7
Langley, A	8	3	3	44	3	0	44	6	0	10	0	3	15	17	0	0	16	50	11	0	0	2	0
Lawler, EE	110	8	115	99	0	1	57	21	1	15	13	44	125	37	54	9	18	17	26	0	1	10	97
Lawrence, PR	17	6	34	317	1	0	188	6	3	62	4	36	459	122	25	3	47	57	81	0	1	14	0
Ledford, GE	16	2	39	19	0	0	10	28	0	3	0	5	12	8	17	1	8	6	3	0	0	1	8
Lewin, K	37	15	42	61	4	40	40	42	0	33	3	81	32	17	35	10	28	30	47	0	1	21	4
Lorsch, JW	14	0	1	32	0	0	25	2	0	12	0	6	62	16	2	1	10	11	16	0	0	4	0
Mathews, J	0	0	2	5	0	2	6	3	0	0	1	2	5	5	0	0	1	1	0	1	0	0	0
Mauborgne, R	4	1	3	6	0	2	3	2	0	1	0	0	8	44	1	0	5	4	2	0	0	0	0
Miller, RH	0	0	0	1	13	14	4	0	0	1	0	3	4	0	0	0	10	2	1	0	0	1	0
Mirvis, P	15	7	10	16	0	2	15	6	1	3	2	19	13	18	25	5	4	9	12	0	0	11	2
Moore, L	0	0	0	5	4	43	2	1	0	2	0	0	0	0	1	0	2	1	0	0	0	0	0
Morrison, EW	18	3	5	29	0	5	19	4	0	7	2	4	6	27	16	0	14	2	3	0	0	1	5
Mouton, JS	1	0	0	0	0	0	2	1	0	1	0	0	2	5	2	1	2	5	0	0	0	0	0
Nelson, RR	6	1	7	215	0	1	244	1	0	20	3	4	116	151	2	0	23	56	25	1	1	1	1
Nohria, N	6	3	6	101	1	1	165	5	0	13	2	3	75	330	3	1	56	30	11	1	0	0	1

Appendix B (Cont.)

Co-citation Counts

	Conger, JA	Cooperrider, D	Cummings, TG	Daft, RL	Davis, DA	DiClemente, CC	DiMaggio, P	Dunphy, D	Eddy, W	Ford, JD	French, JL	French, W	Galbraith, JR	Ghoshal, S	Golembiewski, RT	Goodstein, LD	Gray, B	Greenwood, R	Greiner, L	Greve, MS	Harris, RT	Harrison, Roger	Heneman, RL
O'Reilly, C	55	3	22	229	0	2	137	10	2	38	6	9	107	125	43	3	44	40	27	0	0	10	21
Palmer, I	3	4	0	6	1	0	12	2	0	20	0	1	2	2	1	0	12	8	3	0	0	0	0
Pasmore, WA	10	18	31	12	0	1	3	4	1	2	1	11	11	4	15	1	10	4	6	0	0	3	0
Pettigrew, AM	34	6	24	158	0	0	153	37	0	43	2	32	98	77	15	2	50	153	52	0	0	30	3
Poole, MS	7	7	6	215	2	3	65	15	0	42	1	3	38	21	11	6	26	59	26	0	1	1	1
Porras, JI	7	5	21	18	0	5	7	9	1	8	2	45	11	6	46	9	7	11	14	0	0	10	1
Potter, J	6	5	0	8	0	7	19	2	0	12	0	9	12	5	2	0	11	39	12	0	0	2	0
Powell, WW	18	6	16	239	2	1	2293	8	0	38	2	11	135	242	11	0	133	243	41	0	0	6	4
Prasad, P	2	3	0	12	0	0	18	0	0	1	0	1	4	2	3	0	2	4	1	0	0	0	0
Prochaska, JO	1	1	1	2	48	3976	0	0	0	7	1	2	1	0	2	0	2	20	3	0	0	3	0
Quinn, RW	0	0	0	1	0	0	0	0	0	0	0	0	1	0	0	2	0	1	0	0	0	0	0
Rajagopalan, N	0	1	1	31	0	0	23	4	0	8	0	1	18	16	1	0	9	10	10	0	0	0	0
Reger, R	7	0	2	65	0	1	70	1	0	24	4	3	20	25	3	0	21	17	10	0	0	1	1
Romanelli, E	13	2	5	69	5	2	107	18	0	22	2	4	51	30	2	0	17	47	62	0	0	4	0
Rousseau, D	73	4	39	111	2	2	58	14	1	31	7	8	56	94	43	4	38	22	16	0	0	9	24
Sashkin, M	84	2	11	13	0	0	8	4	0	1	1	18	6	8	13	9	7	6	10	0	0	10	3
Schaffer, RH	1	0	2	4	0	0	4	4	0	4	0	6	2	4	2	2	0	1	4	1	0	2	0
Schein, E	100	29	66	210	6	5	146	46	3	51	6	119	115	102	82	27	79	88	68	0	2	74	9
Sebastian, JG	1	0	0	0	0	5	5	0	0	0	0	0	0	1	0	0	4	47	0	0	0	0	0
Senge, PM	33	8	23	122	5	5	33	15	0	12	2	25	40	54	15	6	16	17	15	0	0	7	1
Shani, R	1	0	0	2	0	0	2	0	0	0	0	2	1	0	0	0	0	0	0	0	0	0	0
Shortell, SM	8	2	4	95	56	8	143	3	0	12	4	9	70	40	4	0	68	42	17	1	0	3	3
Sproull, LS	3	1	4	51	0	2	16	1	0	10	1	2	10	5	2	0	10	9	2	0	0	2	0
Stacey, RD	2	3	6	26	0	1	19	7	0	6	0	7	9	8	0	0	3	13	5	0	0	1	0

Co-citation Counts

	Conger, JA	Cooprider, D	Cummings, TG	Daft, RL	Davis, DA	DiClemente, CC	DiMaggio, P	Dunphy, D	Eddy, W	Ford, JD	French, JL	French, W	Galbraith, JR	Ghoshal, S	Golembiewski, RT	Goodstein, LD	Gray, B	Greenwood, R	Greiner, L	Greve, MS	Harris, RT	Harrison, Roger	Heneman, RL
Stevenson, WB	5	1	1	17	0	0	7	1	0	3	1	1	9	12	3	0	9	6	3	0	0	2	4
Stewart, WH	1	0	0	10	0	0	2	0	0	0	0	2	2	5	0	0	1	0	2	0	0	0	0
Stimpert, JL	4	1	1	37	0	0	32	4	0	21	1	0	8	21	1	0	9	19	7	0	0	0	0
Tannenbaum, R	9	0	4	3	0	0	2	2	1	0	1	7	2	2	6	4	0	1	7	0	0	2	0
Tsoukas, H	7	4	5	64	0	2	45	4	0	22	1	4	13	48	3	0	15	31	12	0	0	3	0
Tushman, M	47	6	33	474	2	2	316	30	0	84	19	16	405	177	15	5	65	163	124	0	0	7	2
Van de Ven, AH	25	11	34	416	0	6	273	23	1	104	23	11	309	199	19	2	149	114	87	0	0	9	9
van Dick, R	1	0	0	1	0	2	0	0	0	0	0	0	1	0	1	0	0	0	0	0	0	1	0
Walton, RE	19	2	71	61	0	0	28	7	1	4	2	40	61	20	29	6	36	8	28	0	0	13	1
Weick, KE	71	29	52	970	3	4	473	26	1	158	8	46	328	209	53	9	152	204	92	0	0	37	11
White, MC	3	0	0	11	0	2	6	1	0	1	0	1	8	2	4	0	1	3	6	0	0	0	1
Winter, SG	1	1	1	67	1	0	70	1	0	3	0	1	35	101	1	0	6	16	7	0	0	1	0
Woodman, R	16	5	17	34	0	2	20	4	1	8	6	23	17	15	28	6	14	18	8	0	0	8	4
Wruck, KH	4	0	0	10	1	0	3	0	0	2	0	0	6	5	0	0	1	1	2	0	0	0	1
Zajac, EJ	15	2	3	118	0	0	226	3	0	20	2	2	69	118	4	0	41	57	33	0	0	0	1

Appendix B (Cont.)

Co-citation Counts

	Hersey, P	Hirschhorn, L	Hornstein, H	Hough, JR	Huff, AS	Huy, QN	Jensen, MC	Kakabadse, A	Kanter, RM	Kiesler, S	Kim, WC	Kotter, J	Langley, A	Lawler, EE	Lawrence, PR	Ledford, GE	Lewin, K	Lorsch, JW	Mathews, J	Mauborgne, R	Miller, RH	Mirvis, P	Moore, L
Adler, NJ	6	3	2	0	7	0	21	1	104	12	26	29	4	29	46	11	28	7	0	0	0	11	4
Alvesson, M	8	15	1	0	22	4	6	2	110	6	4	46	15	27	25	7	43	4	1	3	0	9	2
Argyris, C	60	80	18	0	114	8	67	15	387	100	27	188	22	286	294	37	389	45	7	19	7	58	0
Armenakis, AA	4	1	1	0	9	6	1	1	35	4	3	41	1	20	15	3	38	2	0	23	1	9	1
Bandura, A	29	13	34	0	21	8	45	2	212	115	13	71	7	237	43	40	611	8	6	9	18	29	39
Barr, PS	0	2	0	0	121	3	12	0	14	22	3	7	8	2	8	0	8	9	0	1	0	1	0
Bartlett, CA	2	11	2	0	28	2	68	1	101	15	97	48	9	22	99	1	16	15	2	30	0	6	1
Bartunek, J	8	8	3	0	60	13	12	6	51	33	4	43	18	20	38	15	56	11	0	3	0	16	0
Beckhard, R	5	5	8	0	4	2	4	3	39	0	4	39	3	31	34	7	60	10	0	3	0	13	1
Bedeian, A	10	2	1	0	11	3	10	1	85	6	2	32	2	87	37	6	46	2	1	2	1	20	0
Beer, M	8	7	7	0	15	8	21	7	120	5	6	108	9	134	41	18	75	10	4	5	1	27	1
Beer, S	2	6	0	0	7	0	6	1	23	5	2	13	2	14	30	1	29	1	2	1	0	2	0
Benne, KD	4	1	2	0	0	0	0	1	6	2	0	3	0	5	6	3	30	1	0	0	0	5	0
Bennis, W	60	32	17	0	8	2	8	10	234	20	7	196	3	98	102	14	171	25	1	5	2	21	0
Blake, RR	117	4	15	0	4	0	9	2	64	13	3	32	0	41	105	3	92	8	0	2	1	20	0
Boeker, W	1	0	0	0	43	0	134	1	37	18	15	28	11	4	46	5	8	71	0	5	2	0	0
Bower, JL	3	4	0	1	49	2	61	1	79	18	18	36	26	19	95	1	11	28	0	9	0	2	0
Brown, LD	3	4	2	0	1	1	46	2	27	4	3	7	2	11	27	4	49	2	1	2	20	6	3
Burke, WW	6	1	8	0	2	1	0	2	40	1	0	39	3	40	21	5	46	5	1	0	1	17	0
Bushe, G	0	1	1	0	1	0	3	0	16	3	1	5	1	25	11	9	7	0	0	1	0	7	0
Coch, L	5	1	4	0	6	1	2	1	34	5	0	31	1	63	29	9	103	7	0	0	0	11	0
Cohen, AR	0	2	2	0	1	1	0	1	26	2	1	16	0	12	10	0	12	2	0	0	0	3	1
Conger, JA	44	8	5	0	9	4	14	2	129	7	5	108	8	110	17	16	37	14	0	4	0	15	0
Cooperrider, D	0	3	1	0	7	2	1	2	12	1	2	7	3	8	6	2	15	0	0	1	0	7	0

Appendix B (Cont.)

Co-citation Counts

	Hersey, P	Hirschhorn, L	Hornstein, H	Hough, JR	Huff, AS	Huy, QN	Jensen, MC	Kakabadse, A	Kanter, RM	Kiesler, S	Kim, WC	Kotter, J	Langley, A	Lawler, EE	Lawrence, PR	Ledford, GE	Lewin, K	Lorsch, JW	Mathews, J	Mauborgne, R	Miller, RH	Mirvis, P	Moore, L
Cummings, TG	3	10	4	0	2	1	4	0	59	6	3	32	3	115	34	39	42	1	2	3	0	10	0
Daft, RL	8	22	2	3	128	3	77	2	207	375	16	88	44	99	317	19	61	32	5	6	1	16	5
Davis, DA	0	1	0	0	0	0	3	0	2	2	0	3	3	0	1	0	4	0	0	0	13	0	4
DiClemente, CC	2	1	0	0	1	0	0	0	4	0	0	5	0	0	0	0	40	0	2	0	14	2	43
DiMaggio, P	3	10	0	1	92	4	195	2	217	69	33	52	44	57	188	10	40	25	6	3	4	15	2
Dunphy, D	2	6	1	0	7	3	6	1	44	2	3	32	6	21	6	28	42	2	3	2	0	6	1
Eddy, W	0	1	0	0	0	0	0	0	0	1	0	0	0	1	3	0	0	0	0	0	0	1	0
Ford, JD	2	10	1	0	51	9	14	0	38	29	4	31	10	15	62	3	33	12	1	0	1	3	2
French, JL	0	1	0	0	0	0	7	0	23	4	0	5	0	13	4	0	3	0	0	0	0	2	0
French, W	8	2	10	0	5	1	2	8	39	2	0	45	3	44	36	5	81	6	2	8	3	19	0
Galbraith, JR	7	15	1	1	27	1	84	2	171	54	20	70	15	125	459	12	32	62	5	8	4	13	0
Ghoshal, S	4	5	2	0	45	5	126	2	124	46	116	62	17	37	122	8	17	16	5	44	0	18	0
Golembiewski, RT	6	8	7	0	6	0	2	3	41	7	1	19	0	54	25	17	35	2	0	1	0	25	1
Goodstein, LD	3	1	4	0	0	0	0	0	13	2	1	7	0	9	3	1	10	1	0	0	0	5	0
Gray, B	2	8	3	0	31	2	28	4	103	20	30	29	16	18	47	8	28	10	1	5	10	4	2
Greenwood, R	4	5	0	0	56	8	51	1	67	25	11	41	50	17	57	6	30	11	1	4	2	9	1
Greiner, L	10	1	4	0	17	2	24	7	74	15	4	45	11	26	81	3	47	16	0	2	1	12	0
Greve, MS	0	0	0	0	0	0	4	0	0	0	0	2	0	0	0	0	0	0	1	0	0	0	0
Harris, RT	0	0	0	0	0	0	0	0	1	0	0	0	0	1	1	0	1	0	1	0	0	0	0
Harrison, Roger	5	4	6	0	3	1	3	6	32	1	0	10	2	10	14	1	21	4	0	0	1	11	0
Heneman, RL	1	1	1	0	2	0	10	0	11	3	0	7	0	97	0	8	4	0	0	0	0	2	0
Hersey, P	–	3	7	0	0	1	3	1	35	3	1	44	1	15	14	3	45	3	0	1	1	1	0
Hirschhorn, L	3	–	0	0	7	2	4	3	66	3	1	24	2	26	19	6	18	1	3	0	0	11	0
Hornstein, H	7	0	–	0	0	0	3	0	16	2	0	8	0	11	6	1	18	1	0	0	0	3	0

Appendix B (Cont.)

Co-citation Counts

	Hersey, P	Hirschhorn, L	Hornstein, H	Hough, JR	Huff, AS	Huy, QN	Jensen, MC	Kakabadse, A	Kanter, RM	Kiesler, S	Kim, WC	Kotter, J	Langley, A	Lawler, EE	Lawrence, PR	Ledford, GE	Lewin, K	Lorsch, JW	Mathews, J	Mauborgne, R	Miller, RH	Mirvis, P	Moore, L
Hough, JR	0	0	0	-	0	0	0	0	0	0	0	0	1	0	0	0	0	0	0	0	0	0	0
Huff, AS	0	7	0	0	-	4	31	3	39	45	12	33	18	14	49	1	42	10	0	2	0	3	3
Huy, QN	1	2	0	0	4	-	0	0	15	1	2	14	7	1	4	1	8	0	0	2	0	1	0
Jensen, MC	3	4	3	0	31	0	-	3	94	25	48	47	5	121	101	8	15	202	6	10	7	18	0
Kakabadse, A	1	3	0	0	3	0	3	-	14	1	2	7	2	1	5	0	7	0	14	2	0	0	0
Kanter, RM	35	66	16	0	39	15	94	14	-	70	34	267	21	270	247	37	167	39	5	19	3	75	7
Kiesler, S	3	3	2	0	45	1	25	1	70	-	10	30	4	23	54	1	47	6	0	7	2	8	0
Kim, WC	1	1	0	0	12	2	48	2	34	10	-	13	3	11	23	2	5	6	0	208	1	6	0
Kotter, J	44	24	8	0	33	14	47	7	267	30	13	-	12	98	102	18	102	29	2	8	1	19	1
Langley, A	1	2	0	1	18	7	5	2	21	4	3	12	-	1	13	0	6	3	0	2	0	2	0
Lawler, EE	15	26	11	0	14	1	121	4	270	23	11	98	1	-	125	130	158	37	11	9	0	99	3
Lawrence, PR	14	19	6	0	49	4	101	5	247	54	23	102	13	125	-	14	77	108	4	8	6	14	0
Ledford, GE	3	6	0	0	1	1	8	0	37	1	2	18	0	130	14	-	14	3	3	1	0	11	0
Lewin, K	45	18	18	0	42	8	15	7	167	47	5	102	6	158	77	14	-	10	3	3	2	32	10
Lorsch, JW	3	1	1	0	10	0	202	0	39	6	6	29	3	37	108	3	10	-	1	3	0	3	1
Mathews, J	0	3	0	0	0	0	6	14	5	0	0	2	0	11	4	3	3	1	-	0	1	1	0
Mauborgne, R	1	0	0	0	2	2	10	2	19	7	208	8	2	9	8	1	3	3	0	-	0	4	0
Miller, RH	1	0	0	0	0	0	7	0	3	2	1	1	0	0	6	0	2	0	1	0	-	0	0
Mirvis, P	1	11	3	0	3	1	18	0	75	8	6	19	2	99	14	11	32	3	1	4	0	-	0
Moore, L	0	0	0	0	3	0	0	0	7	0	0	1	0	3	0	0	10	1	0	0	0	0	-
Morrison, EW	1	2	0	0	4	3	20	0	41	16	10	35	4	53	6	9	24	0	1	9	17	12	1
Mouton, JS	9	3	5	0	1	0	3	0	6	2	1	1	0	2	4	0	6	1	0	0	1	11	0
Nelson, RR	0	16	1	2	64	1	222	4	122	68	55	33	11	35	158	3	41	13	6	12	2	5	0
Nohria, N	1	9	0	0	36	3	65	1	97	39	79	36	7	25	88	5	15	12	4	33	0	9	0

Co-citation Counts

	Moore, L	Mirvis, P	Miller, RH	Mauborgne, R	Mathews, J	Lorsch, JW	Lewin, K	Ledford, GE	Lawrence, PR	Lawler, EE	Langley, A	Kotter, J	Kim, WC	Kiesler, S	Kanter, RM	Kakabadse, A	Jensen, MC	Huy, QN	Huff, AS	Hough, JR	Hornstein, H	Hirschhorn, L	Hersey, P
O'Reilly, C	3	43	0	30	1	83	91	31	139	251	12	115	41	114	445	2	234	11	44	0	8	9	15
Palmer, I	0	1	0	1	2	0	5	1	2	2	5	10	1	1	10	0	3	0	5	0	0	3	3
Pasmore, WA	0	22	0	0	3	1	22	13	17	39	0	20	0	4	26	0	1	1	2	0	2	6	2
Pettigrew, AM	2	8	2	8	1	38	88	11	137	43	86	139	13	32	224	15	68	10	109	1	1	15	12
Poole, MS	0	3	2	2	0	5	46	6	41	22	23	30	4	200	65	1	20	9	35	0	2	7	6
Porras, JI	0	28	0	1	0	4	37	9	14	29	4	23	2	1	30	3	2	5	10	0	3	3	2
Potter, J	3	3	1	1	2	0	32	1	2	2	5	9	1	12	17	1	2	0	7	0	1	4	2
Powell, WW	1	18	5	5	5	35	43	12	259	64	37	53	57	61	268	5	247	2	91	1	0	24	2
Prasad, P	1	0	0	0	0	0	5	0	2	1	1	9	0	4	8	2	0	0	2	0	0	0	0
Prochaska, JO	44	3	15	0	2	1	58	0	0	3	0	9	0	9	5	0	1	0	1	0	0	3	5
Quinn, RW	0	0	2	0	0	0	0	0	0	1	0	1	0	1	0	0	2	0	0	0	0	0	0
Rajagopalan, N	0	0	0	6	0	11	5	2	17	11	10	8	20	9	10	3	55	3	20	2	0	2	0
Reger, R	0	2	0	2	0	4	18	3	28	17	9	19	12	26	20	1	26	4	200	0	0	4	2
Romanelli, E	0	1	1	1	0	16	22	5	63	8	22	40	10	29	66	0	47	10	35	0	0	7	3
Rousseau, D	5	59	7	18	0	12	72	35	75	218	7	91	23	45	202	5	62	9	16	1	6	15	5
Sashkin, M	0	13	0	0	2	4	33	11	19	50	0	42	1	3	58	0	2	0	3	0	9	1	26
Schaffer, RH	0	2	0	0	3	0	9	0	6	15	0	14	0	1	9	1	2	0	0	0	2	2	1
Schein, E	6	74	3	10	2	54	338	32	204	224	14	352	17	56	506	12	66	14	59	0	16	65	46
Sebastian, JG	0	0	1	0	0	0	1	0	0	1	0	0	0	1	0	0	0	0	1	0	0	0	1
Senge, PM	1	10	3	7	3	7	45	11	44	56	2	96	10	23	130	5	21	2	39	0	4	29	12
Shani, R	0	0	0	0	1	0	1	3	2	4	0	0	0	0	1	0	0	0	0	0	0	0	1
Shortell, SM	7	0	94	2	1	18	12	8	90	33	20	30	11	12	77	0	71	0	32	0	1	7	1
Sproull, LS	0	7	4	1	0	4	7	1	15	9	0	6	2	228	13	0	3	1	11	0	0	3	1
Stacey, RD	0	6	0	2	1	1	17	1	17	3	9	15	2	1	20	0	5	0	10	0	0	8	2

Appendix B (Cont.)

Co-citation Counts

	Hersey, P	Hirschhorn, L	Hornstein, H	Hough, JR	Huff, AS	Huy, QN	Jensen, MC	Kakabadse, A	Kanter, RM	Kiesler, S	Kim, WC	Kotter, J	Langley, A	Lawler, EE	Lawrence, PR	Ledford, GE	Lewin, K	Lorsch, JW	Mathews, J	Mauborgne, R	Miller, RH	Mirvis, P	Moore, L
Stevenson, WB	1	1	0	1	0	1	13	1	17	5	3	10	1	22	17	1	5	4	0	1	0	2	0
Stewart, WH	0	0	0	0	0	0	6	0	3	1	1	2	2	0	5	0	0	0	1	0	0	0	0
Stimpert, JL	0	2	0	0	117	1	35	0	15	24	13	6	4	17	12	0	7	12	0	2	0	2	0
Tannenbaum, R	34	3	4	0	2	0	0	1	14	3	3	15	1	17	13	1	29	3	0	3	0	5	0
Tsoukas, H	2	7	0	0	27	4	13	0	29	10	7	17	29	6	21	3	20	1	0	6	3	3	0
Tushman, M	10	24	2	1	119	16	129	5	325	131	49	137	54	82	378	20	85	56	2	22	3	13	0
Van de Ven, AH	4	22	3	1	101	8	105	2	341	67	58	92	60	107	360	21	82	31	7	18	4	16	0
van Dick, R	0	0	0	0	0	1	0	0	2	2	1	2	0	0	0	0	6	0	0	1	0	2	0
Walton, RE	9	35	11	0	4	0	33	3	141	22	8	50	4	214	118	49	69	9	2	6	0	40	3
Weick, KE	24	69	6	1	254	15	126	3	461	235	47	216	76	189	502	31	223	58	2	29	6	57	3
White, MC	6	1	0	0	5	0	7	1	38	9	3	8	0	3	10	0	1	6	0	1	0	1	1
Winter, SG	0	2	0	0	20	1	78	1	26	10	27	4	6	15	55	0	7	2	2	7	0	5	0
Woodman, R	2	1	3	0	15	2	5	0	84	6	4	23	17	45	18	8	33	2	0	3	1	21	0
Wruck, KH	0	0	0	0	2	0	324	0	5	5	1	12	1	13	3	0	1	34	3	1	1	1	0
Zajac, EJ	0	4	0	0	83	1	296	2	82	34	37	31	17	39	89	6	10	96	1	8	2	7	0

Appendix B (Cont.)

Co-citation Counts

	Morrison, EW	Mouton, JS	Nelson, RR	Nohria, N	O'Reilly, C	Palmer, I	Pasmore, WA	Pettigrew, AM	Poole, MS	Porras, JI	Potter, J	Powell, WW	Prasad, P	Prochaska, JO	Quinn, RW	Rajagopalan, N	Reger, R	Romanelli, E	Rousseau, D	Sashkin, M	Schaffer, RH	Schein, E	Sebastian, JG
Adler, NJ	9	3	15	37	75	0	4	13	25	4	5	54	1	0	0	1	4	6	41	11	0	93	0
Alvesson, M	15	7	30	26	23	44	10	119	31	3	68	81	19	0	0	2	8	8	45	6	2	164	0
Argyris, C	71	7	239	80	117	12	32	232	86	61	17	186	15	11	0	12	36	58	159	55	17	773	1
Armenakis, AA	6	0	4	1	34	3	9	18	13	28	1	4	0	5	1	0	5	3	32	7	0	39	0
Bandura, A	98	5	111	15	248	2	14	30	40	32	40	64	2	1620	1	7	15	13	168	33	5	213	0
Barr, PS	3	0	22	4	14	1	1	22	15	4	0	29	0	1	0	8	29	15	3	0	0	20	0
Bartlett, CA	14	1	92	231	59	3	13	47	14	5	6	130	2	0	0	12	18	20	32	5	2	71	0
Bartunek, J	14	1	26	7	44	5	7	84	33	25	9	55	5	1	1	6	24	34	31	7	0	112	0
Beckhard, R	2	1	4	2	8	0	6	28	7	30	0	9	0	1	0	2	2	11	6	15	3	117	1
Bedeian, A	33	0	9	4	124	1	16	21	15	15	1	13	0	1	0	4	8	7	121	10	1	78	0
Beer, M	14	0	18	37	51	3	4	71	18	59	5	34	0	3	0	4	12	19	32	27	21	159	0
Beer, S	4	0	18	4	4	0	1	21	4	1	1	12	0	0	0	0	2	1	4	0	1	38	0
Benne, KD	0	0	0	0	7	0	12	3	11	2	0	0	0	1	0	0	0	0	1	0	0	21	0
Bennis, W	10	4	15	12	52	3	7	86	32	32	5	37	3	3	0	1	8	19	47	78	5	306	0
Blake, RR	3	41	3	2	28	2	0	19	17	17	0	7	0	2	0	0	0	3	25	27	0	106	0
Boeker, W	6	0	81	33	116	3	1	58	11	0	0	129	0	0	0	39	27	102	14	0	1	35	1
Bower, JL	6	1	133	35	44	1	12	97	12	0	0	72	0	0	0	13	23	33	8	4	1	45	0
Brown, LD	6	0	8	5	20	3	13	10	5	7	3	24	3	1	0	1	1	2	7	2	0	23	0
Burke, WW	0	0	2	6	9	2	6	18	4	42	0	3	0	2	0	0	2	0	11	39	3	73	0
Bushe, G	0	0	1	2	6	0	10	4	1	5	0	2	0	1	0	0	5	0	6	6	0	20	0
Coch, L	3	1	8	4	8	0	2	8	4	12	3	4	1	1	0	0	1	4	10	19	1	49	0
Cohen, AR	3	1	2	0	21	1	10	3	1	4	1	1	1	1	0	0	1	2	5	0	0	9	0
Conger, JA	18	1	6	6	55	3	10	34	7	7	6	18	2	1	0	0	7	13	73	84	1	100	1
Cooperrider, D	3	0	1	3	3	4	18	6	7	5	5	6	3	1	0	1	0	2	4	2	0	29	0

76

Appendix B (Cont.)

Co-citation Counts

	Morrison, EW	Mouton, JS	Nelson, RR	Nohria, N	O'Reilly, C	Palmer, I	Pasmore, WA	Pettigrew, AM	Poole, MS	Porras, JI	Potter, J	Powell, WW	Prasad, P	Prochaska, JO	Quinn, RW	Rajagopalan, N	Reger, R	Romanelli, E	Rousseau, D	Sashkin, M	Schaffer, RH	Schein, E	Sebastian, JG
Cummings, TG	5	0	7	6	22	0	31	24	6	21	0	16	0	1	0	1	2	5	39	11	2	66	0
Daft, RL	29	1	215	101	229	6	12	158	215	18	8	239	12	2	1	31	65	69	111	13	4	210	0
Davis, DA	0	0	0	1	0	1	0	0	2	0	0	2	0	48	0	0	0	2	5	2	0	6	0
DiClemente, CC	5	0	1	1	2	0	1	0	3	5	7	1	0	3976	0	0	1	0	2	0	0	5	5
DiMaggio, P	19	2	244	165	137	12	3	153	65	7	19	2293	18	0	0	23	70	107	58	8	4	146	0
Dunphy, D	4	1	1	5	10	2	4	37	15	9	2	8	0	0	0	4	1	18	14	4	0	46	0
Eddy, W	0	0	0	0	2	0	1	0	0	1	0	0	0	0	0	0	0	0	0	1	0	3	0
Ford, JD	7	1	20	13	38	20	2	43	42	8	12	38	1	7	0	8	24	22	31	0	0	51	0
French, JL	2	0	3	2	6	1	1	2	1	2	1	0	0	0	0	0	4	2	7	1	0	6	0
French, W	4	0	4	3	9	0	11	32	3	45	1	11	1	2	0	1	3	4	8	18	6	119	0
Galbraith, JR	6	2	116	75	107	2	11	98	38	11	1	135	4	1	0	18	20	51	56	6	2	115	0
Ghoshal, S	27	5	151	330	125	2	4	77	21	6	5	242	2	0	1	16	25	30	94	8	4	102	1
Golembiewski, RT	16	2	2	3	43	1	15	15	11	46	2	11	3	2	0	1	3	2	43	13	2	82	0
Goodstein, LD	0	1	0	0	3	0	1	2	6	9	0	0	0	0	0	2	0	0	4	9	2	27	0
Gray, B	14	2	23	56	44	12	10	50	26	7	11	133	2	0	0	9	21	17	38	7	0	79	4
Greenwood, R	2	5	56	30	40	8	4	153	59	11	39	243	4	20	1	10	17	47	22	6	1	88	47
Greiner, L	3	0	25	11	27	3	6	52	26	14	12	41	1	3	0	10	10	62	16	10	4	68	0
Greve, MS	0	0	1	1	0	0	0	0	0	0	0	0	0	0	0	0	0	0	0	0	0	1	0
Harris, RT	0	0	1	0	0	0	0	0	0	1	0	0	0	0	0	0	0	0	0	0	0	2	0
Harrison, Roger	1	0	1	0	10	0	3	30	1	10	2	6	0	3	0	0	1	4	9	10	2	74	0
Heneman, RL	5	0	0	1	21	0	0	3	1	1	0	4	0	0	0	1	0	1	24	3	0	9	0
Hersey, P	1	9	0	1	15	3	2	12	6	2	2	2	0	5	0	0	2	3	5	26	1	46	1
Hirschhorn, L	2	3	16	9	9	3	6	15	7	3	4	24	0	3	0	2	4	7	15	1	2	65	0
Hornstein, H	5	0	1	0	8	0	2	1	2	3	1	0	0	0	0	0	0	0	6	9	2	16	0

Appendix B (Cont.)

Co-citation Counts

	Morrison, EW	Mouton, JS	Nelson, RR	Nohria, N	O'Reilly, C	Palmer, I	Pasmore, WA	Pettigrew, AM	Poole, MS	Porras, JI	Potter, J	Powell, WW	Prasad, P	Prochaska, JO	Quinn, RW	Rajagopalan, N	Reger, R	Romanelli, E	Rousseau, D	Sashkin, M	Schaffer, RH	Schein, E	Sebastian, JG
Hough, JR	0	0	2	0	0	0	0	1	0	0	0	1	0	0	0	2	0	0	1	0	0	0	0
Huff, AS	4	1	64	36	44	5	2	109	35	10	7	91	2	1	0	20	200	35	16	3	0	59	1
Huy, QN	3	0	1	3	11	0	1	10	9	5	0	2	0	0	0	3	4	10	9	0	0	14	0
Jensen, MC	20	3	222	65	234	3	1	68	20	2	2	247	0	1	2	55	26	47	62	2	2	66	0
Kakabadse, A	0	0	4	1	2	0	0	15	1	3	1	5	2	0	0	3	1	0	5	0	1	12	0
Kanter, RM	41	6	122	97	445	10	26	224	65	30	17	268	8	5	0	10	20	66	202	58	9	506	1
Kiesler, S	16	2	68	39	114	1	4	32	200	1	12	61	4	9	1	9	26	29	45	3	1	56	0
Kim, WC	10	1	55	79	41	1	0	13	4	2	1	57	0	0	0	20	12	10	23	0	1	17	0
Kotter, J	35	1	33	36	115	10	20	139	30	23	9	53	1	9	1	8	19	40	91	42	14	352	1
Langley, A	4	0	11	7	12	5	0	86	23	4	5	37	1	0	0	10	9	22	7	2	0	14	0
Lawler, EE	53	2	35	25	251	2	39	43	22	29	2	64	1	3	1	11	17	8	218	50	15	224	1
Lawrence, PR	6	4	158	88	139	2	17	137	41	14	2	259	2	0	0	17	28	63	75	19	6	204	0
Ledford, GE	9	0	3	5	31	1	13	11	6	9	1	12	3	0	0	2	3	5	35	11	1	32	0
Lewin, K	24	6	41	15	91	5	22	88	46	37	32	43	5	58	0	5	18	22	72	33	9	338	1
Lorsch, JW	0	1	13	12	83	0	1	38	5	4	0	35	0	1	0	11	4	16	12	4	0	54	0
Mathews, J	1	0	6	4	4	2	3	1	0	0	2	5	0	2	0	0	1	0	0	2	3	2	0
Mauborgne, R	9	0	12	33	30	0	0	8	2	1	0	5	0	0	0	6	2	1	18	0	1	10	0
Miller, RH	17	1	2	1	0	0	0	2	2	1	1	5	0	15	2	0	0	1	7	0	0	3	1
Mirvis, P	12	11	5	9	43	1	22	8	8	28	3	18	3	3	0	0	2	1	59	13	2	74	0
Moore, L	1	0	0	0	3	0	0	2	0	0	3	1	1	0	0	0	0	0	5	0	0	6	0
Morrison, EW	-	0	10	10	114	1	3	13	11	2	5	28	0	3	0	2	6	5	202	3	2	139	1
Mouton, JS	0	-	1	0	6	0	0	1	0	0	1	4	0	0	0	0	0	0	3	0	0	4	0
Nelson, RR	10	0	-	107	66	2	3	82	47	6	1	438	3	1	1	15	32	91	32	3	5	93	2
Nohria, N	10	0	107	-	77	5	2	54	30	2	4	336	3	1	0	19	29	20	42	2	2	64	2

Appendix B (Cont.)

Co-citation Counts

	Morrison, EW	Mouton, JS	Nelson, RR	Nohria, N	O'Reilly, C	Palmer, I	Pasmore, WA	Pettigrew, AM	Poole, MS	Porras, JI	Potter, J	Powell, WW	Prasad, P	Prochaska, JO	Quinn, RW	Rajagopalan, N	Reger, R	Romanelli, E	Rousseau, D	Sashkin, M	Schaffer, RH	Schein, E	Sebastian, JG
O'Reilly, C	114	6	66	77	-	2	10	103	75	16	2	154	4	3	0	34	32	75	322	27	6	360	1
Palmer, I	1	0	2	5	2	-	1	17	6	0	15	9	1	1	0	0	4	2	3	1	0	12	0
Pasmore, WA	3	1	3	2	10	1	-	9	14	18	2	4	13	1	0	0	0	4	12	10	0	26	0
Pettigrew, AM	13	0	82	54	103	17	9	-	83	13	14	156	19	1	0	25	35	69	55	20	6	287	0
Poole, MS	11	0	47	30	75	6	14	83	-	11	8	72	0	4	0	4	21	27	31	1	1	72	0
Porras, JI	2	0	6	2	16	15	18	13	11	-	0	9	3	6	0	3	5	5	11	17	1	49	0
Potter, J	5	0	1	4	2	15	2	14	8	0	-	15	16	12	0	1	2	0	7	3	0	13	0
Powell, WW	28	4	438	336	154	9	4	156	72	9	15	-	16	1	0	27	71	108	103	8	4	160	6
Prasad, P	0	0	0	3	4	1	13	13	4	0	3	16	-	0	0	0	1	1	4	0	0	17	0
Prochaska, JO	3	0	1	1	3	1	1	1	4	6	12	1	0	-	0	0	1	3	3	0	0	9	0
Quinn, RW	0	0	0	0	0	0	0	0	0	0	0	0	0	0	-	0	0	0	1	0	0	0	0
Rajagopalan, N	2	0	15	19	34	0	0	25	4	0	0	27	0	0	0	-	14	19	8	0	0	11	0
Reger, R	6	0	32	29	32	4	0	35	21	3	2	71	1	1	0	14	-	23	15	5	5	38	1
Romanelli, E	5	0	91	20	75	2	4	69	27	5	5	108	1	3	0	19	23	-	30	6	1	48	0
Rousseau, D	202	3	32	42	322	3	12	55	31	5	0	103	4	3	1	8	15	30	-	26	2	323	0
Sashkin, M	3	0	3	2	2	2	10	20	1	17	7	8	0	0	0	0	5	6	26	-	4	64	0
Schaffer, RH	2	0	5	2	6	0	0	6	1	1	3	4	0	0	0	0	5	1	2	4	-	13	1
Schein, E	139	4	93	64	360	12	26	287	72	49	13	160	17	9	0	11	38	48	323	64	13	-	1
Sebastian, JG	1	0	2	2	1	0	0	0	0	0	0	6	0	0	0	0	1	0	0	0	0	1	-
Senge, PM	12	2	86	45	26	8	12	45	31	17	0	69	1	9	1	6	16	12	26	18	9	223	0
Shani, R	0	0	1	1	0	0	0	1	0	0	0	2	0	0	0	0	6	0	0	0	5	2	0
Shortell, SM	25	0	39	43	62	4	3	39	21	3	4	161	2	18	0	29	38	24	236	3	4	58	4
Sproull, LS	2	1	17	2	23	1	2	20	15	1	3	15	1	1	0	0	7	3	10	1	0	28	0
Stacey, RD	3	0	25	12	4	1	3	25	12	3	2	18	0	1	0	5	1	12	6	4	1	24	0

Co-citation Counts

	Sebastian, JG	Schein, E	Schaffer, RH	Sashkin, M	Rousseau, D	Romanelli, E	Reger, R	Rajagopalan, N	Quinn, RW	Prochaska, JO	Prasad, P	Powell, WW	Potter, J	Porras, JI	Poole, MS	Pettigrew, AM	Pasmore, WA	Palmer, I	O'Reilly, C	Nohria, N	Nelson, RR	Mouton, JS	Morrison, EW
Stevenson, WB	0	11	0	1	7	3	2	5	0	0	0	13	0	1	3	14	1	0	17	13	9	0	4
Stewart, WH	0	4	0	0	1	4	0	2	0	0	0	2	1	0	1	2	0	0	5	1	5	0	0
Stimpert, JL	0	12	0	0	3	16	64	15	0	0	0	31	1	3	11	21	0	1	12	14	27	0	2
Tannenbaum, R	0	23	1	7	4	2	1	1	0	0	0	3	2	7	0	5	3	1	4	0	0	1	2
Tsoukas, H	0	40	0	0	10	12	12	3	1	2	6	59	12	5	45	57	5	20	14	35	51	1	6
Tushman, M	0	228	9	24	107	425	76	45	1	3	6	412	3	21	119	267	15	3	333	146	546	0	24
Van de Ven, AH	1	181	3	13	171	130	56	35	1	7	4	459	8	13	303	230	18	13	162	207	272	3	28
van Dick, R	0	1	0	0	12	0	1	0	0	1	0	0	0	1	0	0	0	0	4	0	0	1	2
Walton, RE	0	124	1	24	64	6	4	1	0	0	2	40	0	28	35	41	30	3	68	14	26	2	7
Weick, KE	1	573	10	32	246	119	115	41	3	5	21	531	47	34	246	408	28	34	343	133	371	5	66
White, MC	0	9	0	0	5	12	2	10	0	1	0	8	1	1	2	10	0	1	18	1	3	0	3
Winter, SG	1	34	2	0	10	30	10	6	0	0	2	134	0	0	11	23	2	0	26	50	628	0	4
Woodman, R	0	50	1	13	36	9	6	4	1	2	1	12	1	34	28	53	15	4	50	8	19	3	6
Wruck, KH	0	3	1	2	2	13	2	6	0	0	0	5	0	0	0	1	0	1	27	2	10	0	2
Zajac, EJ	3	38	0	1	40	75	76	75	0	0	2	275	2	1	23	79	3	4	165	94	119	0	6

Appendix B (Cont.)

Co-citation Counts

	Senge, PM	Shani, R	Shortell, SM	Sproull, LS	Stacey, RD	Stevenson, WB	Stewart, WH	Stimpert, JL	Tannenbaum, R	Tsoukas, H	Tushman, M	Van de Ven, AH	van Dick, R	Walton, RE	Weick, KE	White, MC	Winter, SG	Woodman, R	Wruck, KH	Zajac, EJ
Adler, NJ	11	1	2	0	1	8	1	2	5	5	27	44	0	25	57	1	3	5	0	16
Alvesson, M	29	0	14	7	15	5	0	2	4	102	26	64	0	9	231	1	13	7	0	9
Argyris, C	486	3	45	26	67	5	4	36	36	87	286	263	1	144	644	6	98	59	5	46
Armenakis, AA	12	0	7	4	2	1	0	4	2	4	16	24	0	9	34	2	0	20	0	3
Bandura, A	63	0	35	10	1	6	10	56	12	8	73	76	5	58	252	15	9	48	3	31
Barr, PS	15	0	15	3	6	0	0	107	0	4	47	42	0	1	80	4	5	5	1	32
Bartlett, CA	35	0	16	4	6	5	1	14	2	11	117	105	0	16	116	0	52	10	2	43
Bartunek, J	32	1	11	14	4	5	0	12	5	31	91	71	0	34	207	2	7	24	0	19
Beckhard, R	17	1	2	1	3	0	0	1	9	3	22	14	1	41	33	1	0	12	0	2
Bedeian, A	12	0	7	5	4	4	0	5	2	8	28	44	0	11	68	9	4	21	2	7
Beer, M	64	2	17	1	12	4	1	6	8	11	62	36	0	79	93	2	5	46	2	7
Beer, S	46	2	7	0	12	4	4	0	2	32	15	20	0	6	74	0	5	0	1	1
Benne, KD	3	0	0	1	0	0	0	0	2	0	4	9	0	10	8	0	0	1	0	1
Bennis, W	59	1	15	5	8	6	2	1	26	10	76	57	0	76	160	6	2	29	2	3
Blake, RR	11	0	6	3	0	3	1	1	34	2	16	20	1	125	42	2	1	12	3	3
Boeker, W	9	0	56	0	5	5	2	29	0	5	175	70	0	5	76	8	26	6	24	179
Bower, JL	23	0	20	5	5	1	2	11	4	6	220	93	0	13	148	4	52	10	4	41
Brown, LD	7	0	36	2	0	0	1	0	0	1	15	23	0	39	29	0	1	8	1	9
Burke, WW	23	0	4	0	3	0	0	0	7	3	16	10	1	31	17	0	0	25	0	1
Bushe, G	5	3	2	1	1	1	0	0	1	2	8	6	0	11	11	0	0	8	0	0
Coch, L	5	0	2	2	0	2	0	1	0	0	21	10	0	16	24	0	0	9	0	2
Cohen, AR	2	0	0	1	0	2	0	1	9	2	8	1	0	8	11	0	0	1	0	3
Conger, JA	33	1	8	3	2	5	1	4	9	7	47	25	1	19	71	3	1	16	4	15
Cooperrider, D	8	0	2	1	3	1	0	1	0	4	6	11	0	2	29	0	1	5	0	2

Appendix B (Cont.)

Co-citation Counts

	Senge, PM	Shani, R	Shortell, SM	Sproull, LS	Stacey, RD	Stevenson, WB	Stewart, WH	Stimpert, JL	Tannenbaum, R	Tsoukas, H	Tushman, M	Van de Ven, AH	van Dick, R	Walton, RE	Weick, KE	White, MC	Winter, SG	Woodman, R	Wruck, KH	Zajac, EJ
Cummings, TG	23	0	4	4	6	1	0	1	4	5	33	34	0	71	52	0	1	17	0	3
Daft, RL	122	2	95	51	26	17	10	37	3	64	474	416	1	61	970	11	67	34	10	118
Davis, DA	5	0	56	0	0	0	0	0	0	0	0	2	0	0	3	0	1	0	1	0
DiClemente, CC	5	0	8	2	1	1	0	0	0	2	2	6	2	0	4	2	0	2	0	0
DiMaggio, P	33	2	143	16	19	7	2	32	2	45	316	273	0	28	473	6	70	20	3	226
Dunphy, D	15	0	3	1	7	1	0	4	2	4	30	23	0	7	26	1	1	4	0	3
Eddy, W	0	0	0	0	0	0	0	0	1	0	0	1	0	1	1	0	0	1	0	0
Ford, JD	12	0	12	10	6	3	0	21	0	22	84	104	0	4	158	1	3	8	2	20
French, JL	2	0	4	1	0	1	0	1	1	1	19	23	0	2	8	0	0	6	0	2
French, W	25	2	9	2	7	1	2	0	7	4	16	11	0	40	46	1	1	23	0	2
Galbraith, JR	40	1	70	10	9	9	2	8	2	13	405	309	1	61	328	8	35	17	6	69
Ghoshal, S	54	0	40	5	8	12	5	21	6	48	177	199	0	20	209	2	101	15	5	118
Golembiewski, RT	15	0	4	2	0	3	0	1	6	3	15	19	1	29	53	4	1	28	0	4
Goodstein, LD	6	0	2	0	0	0	0	0	4	0	5	2	0	6	9	0	0	6	0	0
Gray, B	16	0	68	10	3	9	1	9	0	15	65	149	0	36	152	1	6	14	1	41
Greenwood, R	17	0	42	9	13	6	6	19	1	31	163	114	0	8	204	3	16	18	1	57
Greiner, L	15	0	17	2	5	3	2	7	7	12	124	87	0	28	92	6	7	8	2	33
Greve, MS	0	0	0	0	0	0	0	0	0	0	0	0	0	0	0	0	0	0	0	0
Harris, RT	0	0	0	0	0	0	0	0	0	0	0	0	0	0	0	0	0	0	0	0
Harrison, Roger	7	0	3	2	1	2	0	0	2	3	7	9	1	13	37	0	1	8	0	0
Heneman, RL	1	0	1	0	0	4	0	0	0	0	2	9	0	1	11	1	0	4	0	0
Hersey, P	12	1	7	1	2	2	6	0	34	2	10	4	0	9	24	6	0	2	0	0
Hirschhorn, L	29	0	7	3	8	1	1	2	3	7	24	22	0	35	69	1	2	1	0	4
Hornstein, H	4	0	1	0	0	0	0	0	4	0	2	3	0	11	6	0	0	3	0	0

Co-citation Counts

	Senge, PM	Shani, R	Shortell, SM	Sproull, LS	Stacey, RD	Stevenson, WB	Stewart, WH	Stimpert, JL	Tannenbaum, R	Tsoukas, H	Tushman, M	Van de Ven, AH	van Dick, R	Walton, RE	Weick, KE	White, MC	Winter, SG	Woodman, R	Wruck, KH	Zajac, EJ
Hough, JR	0	0	0	0	0	1	0	0	0	0	1	1	0	0	1	0	0	0	0	0
Huff, AS	39	0	32	11	10	0	0	117	2	27	119	101	0	4	254	5	20	15	2	83
Huy, QN	2	0	0	1	0	0	0	1	1	4	16	8	1	1	15	0	1	2	0	1
Jensen, MC	21	0	71	3	5	13	6	35	0	13	129	105	0	33	126	7	78	5	324	296
Kakabadse, A	5	0	0	0	0	1	0	0	1	0	5	2	0	3	3	1	1	0	0	2
Kanter, RM	130	1	77	13	20	17	3	15	14	29	325	341	2	141	461	38	26	84	5	82
Kiesler, S	23	0	12	228	1	5	1	24	3	10	131	67	2	22	235	9	10	6	5	34
Kim, WC	10	0	11	1	2	3	1	13	3	7	49	58	1	8	47	3	27	4	1	37
Kotter, J	96	2	30	6	15	10	2	6	15	17	137	92	2	50	216	8	4	23	12	31
Langley, A	2	0	20	0	9	1	2	4	1	29	54	60	0	4	76	0	6	17	1	17
Lawler, EE	56	4	33	9	3	22	0	2	17	6	82	107	0	214	189	3	15	45	13	39
Lawrence, PR	44	2	90	15	17	17	5	12	13	21	378	360	0	118	502	10	55	18	3	89
Ledford, GE	11	3	8	1	1	1	0	0	1	3	20	21	0	49	31	0	0	8	0	6
Lewin, K	45	1	12	7	17	5	0	7	29	20	85	82	6	69	223	1	7	33	1	10
Lorsch, JW	7	0	18	4	1	4	0	12	3	1	56	31	0	9	58	6	2	2	34	96
Mathews, J	3	1	1	0	1	0	1	0	0	0	2	7	0	2	2	0	2	0	3	1
Mauborgne, R	7	0	2	1	2	1	0	2	3	6	22	18	1	6	29	1	7	3	1	8
Miller, RH	3	0	94	4	0	0	0	0	0	0	3	4	0	0	6	0	0	1	1	2
Mirvis, P	10	0	7	0	6	2	0	2	5	3	13	16	2	40	57	1	5	21	1	7
Moore, L	1	0	7	0	0	0	0	0	0	0	0	0	0	0	3	1	0	0	0	0
Morrison, EW	12	0	25	2	3	4	0	2	2	6	24	28	2	7	66	3	4	6	2	6
Mouton, JS	2	0	0	1	0	0	0	0	1	1	0	3	1	2	5	0	0	3	0	0
Nelson, RR	86	1	39	17	25	9	5	27	0	51	546	272	0	26	371	3	628	19	10	119
Nohria, N	45	1	43	2	12	13	1	14	0	35	146	207	0	14	133	1	50	8	2	94

Appendix B (Cont.)

Co-citation Counts

	Senge, PM	Shani, R	Shortell, SM	Sproull, LS	Stacey, RD	Stevenson, WB	Stewart, WH	Stimpert, JL	Tannenbaum, R	Tsoukas, H	Tushman, M	Van de Ven, AH	van Dick, R	Walton, RE	Weick, KE	White, MC	Winter, SG	Woodman, R	Wruck, KH	Zajac, EJ
O'Reilly, C	26	0	62	23	4	17	5	12	4	14	333	162	4	68	343	18	26	50	27	165
Palmer, I	8	0	4	1	1	0	0	1	1	20	3	13	0	3	34	1	0	4	1	4
Pasmore, WA	12	0	3	2	3	1	0	0	3	5	15	18	0	30	28	0	2	15	0	3
Pettigrew, AM	45	1	39	20	25	14	2	21	5	57	267	230	0	41	408	10	23	53	1	79
Poole, MS	31	0	21	15	12	3	1	11	0	45	119	303	0	35	246	2	11	28	0	23
Porras, JI	17	0	3	1	3	0	0	3	7	5	21	13	1	28	34	1	0	34	0	1
Potter, J	0	0	4	3	2	1	1	1	2	12	3	8	0	1	47	0	0	1	0	2
Powell, WW	69	2	161	15	18	13	2	31	3	59	412	459	0	40	531	8	134	12	5	275
Prasad, P	1	0	2	1	0	0	0	0	0	6	6	4	0	2	21	0	2	1	0	2
Prochaska, JO	9	0	18	1	1	0	0	0	0	2	3	7	1	0	5	1	0	2	0	0
Quinn, RW	1	0	0	0	0	0	0	0	0	0	1	1	0	0	3	0	0	1	0	0
Rajagopalan, N	6	0	29	0	5	5	2	15	1	3	45	35	0	1	41	10	6	4	6	75
Reger, R	16	6	38	7	1	2	0	64	1	12	76	56	1	4	115	2	10	6	2	76
Romanelli, E	12	0	24	3	12	3	4	16	2	12	425	130	0	6	119	12	30	9	13	75
Rousseau, D	26	0	236	10	6	7	1	3	4	10	107	171	12	64	246	5	10	36	2	40
Sashkin, M	18	0	3	1	4	1	0	0	7	0	24	13	0	24	32	0	0	13	2	1
Schaffer, RH	9	5	4	0	1	0	0	0	1	0	9	3	0	1	10	0	2	1	1	0
Schein, E	223	2	58	28	24	11	4	12	23	40	228	181	1	124	573	9	34	50	3	38
Sebastian, JG	0	0	4	0	0	0	0	0	0	0	0	1	0	0	1	0	1	0	0	3
Senge, PM	-	1	26	2	41	1	1	13	0	29	88	78	1	24	244	1	40	14	1	20
Shani, R	1	-	1	0	0	0	0	0	0	0	1	1	0	2	3	0	1	0	1	0
Shortell, SM	26	1	-	2	12	4	3	17	0	8	104	98	5	9	146	1	18	9	7	287
Sproull, LS	2	0	2	-	0	0	0	2	0	6	24	13	0	5	65	0	3	2	0	4
Stacey, RD	41	0	12	0	-	1	1	5	0	22	36	32	0	2	71	3	3	2	1	6

Co-citation Counts

	Zajac, EJ	Wruck, KH	Woodman, R	Winter, SG	White, MC	Weick, KE	Walton, RE	van Dick, R	Van de Ven, AH	Tushman, M	Tsoukas, H	Tannenbaum, R	Stimpert, JL	Stewart, WH	Stevenson, WB	Stacey, RD	Sproull, LS	Shortell, SM	Shani, R	Senge, PM
Stevenson, WB	15	1	1	4	1	23	7	0	11	20	3	0	0	0	-	1	0	4	0	1
Stewart, WH	3	0	0	0	0	10	0	0	9	3	1	0	0	-	0	1	0	3	0	1
Stimpert, JL	48	2	4	5	0	65	1	0	42	46	5	0	-	0	0	5	2	17	0	13
Tannenbaum, R	1	0	4	0	0	12	11	0	2	4	0	-	0	0	0	0	0	0	0	0
Tsoukas, H	13	1	14	31	1	202	4	0	65	58	-	0	5	1	3	22	6	8	0	29
Tushman, M	201	24	42	156	20	583	63	0	569	-	58	4	46	3	20	36	24	104	1	88
Van de Ven, AH	170	8	63	88	8	553	74	0	-	569	65	2	42	9	11	32	13	98	1	78
van Dick, R	0	0	0	0	0	4	0	-	0	0	0	0	0	0	0	0	0	5	0	1
Walton, RE	15	2	19	8	1	117	-	0	74	63	4	11	1	0	7	2	5	9	2	24
Weick, KE	178	13	63	131	13	-	117	4	553	583	202	12	65	10	23	71	65	146	3	244
White, MC	19	5	2	0	-	13	1	0	8	20	1	0	0	1	1	1	1	1	0	1
Winter, SG	41	11	5	-	0	131	8	0	88	156	31	0	5	0	4	3	3	18	1	40
Woodman, R	10	0	-	5	2	63	19	0	63	42	14	4	4	0	1	2	2	9	0	14
Wruck, KH	31	-	0	11	5	13	2	0	8	24	1	0	2	0	1	1	0	7	1	1
Zajac, EJ	-	31	10	41	19	178	15	0	170	201	13	1	48	3	15	6	4	287	0	20

Appendix C

Co-citation Correlation Matrix

	Adler, NJ	Alvesson, M	Argyris, C	Armenakis, AA	Bandura, A	Barr, PS	Bartlett, CA	Bartunek, J	Beckhard, R	Bedeian, A	Beer, M	Beer, S	Benne, KD
Adler, NJ	1.000												
Alvesson, M	0.408	1.000											
Argyris, C	0.446	0.644	1.000										
Armenakis, AA	0.144	0.130	0.206	1.000									
Bandura, A	0.143	0.057	0.163	0.104	1.000								
Barr, PS	0.124	0.243	0.304	0.015	-0.007	1.000							
Bartlett, CA	0.657	0.217	0.232	-0.019	-0.020	0.141	1.000						
Bartunek, J	0.333	0.616	0.713	0.190	0.085	0.416	0.181	1.000					
Beckhard, R	0.221	0.291	0.622	0.200	0.052	0.010	0.031	0.363	1.000				
Bedeian, A	0.366	0.257	0.372	0.840	0.197	0.066	0.075	0.298	0.228	1.000			
Beer, M	0.403	0.438	0.736	0.277	0.100	0.116	0.149	0.485	0.735	0.387	1.000		
Beer, S	0.238	0.523	0.742	0.088	0.045	0.217	0.157	0.530	0.381	0.179	0.436	1.000	
Benne, KD	0.188	0.214	0.514	0.141	0.134	0.007	-0.023	0.303	0.614	0.196	0.438	0.297	1.000
Bennis, W	0.387	0.451	0.772	0.226	0.145	0.082	0.105	0.480	0.774	0.337	0.717	0.478	0.628
Blake, RR	0.278	0.233	0.569	0.138	0.126	-0.016	0.008	0.323	0.640	0.230	0.544	0.334	0.671
Boeker, W	0.247	0.178	0.218	-0.004	-0.013	0.359	0.234	0.285	-0.007	0.113	0.099	0.118	-0.029
Bower, JL	0.350	0.369	0.481	0.046	0.002	0.369	0.447	0.463	0.120	0.166	0.262	0.375	0.073
Brown, LD	0.243	0.289	0.485	0.069	0.064	0.088	0.078	0.419	0.349	0.151	0.373	0.352	0.437
Burke, WW	0.215	0.251	0.568	0.301	0.069	-0.045	-0.017	0.298	0.759	0.321	0.780	0.286	0.504
Bushe, G	0.320	0.298	0.562	0.227	0.074	0.050	0.069	0.358	0.524	0.372	0.634	0.322	0.324
Coch, L	0.203	0.248	0.580	0.247	0.197	0.043	0.002	0.334	0.533	0.318	0.582	0.345	0.510
Cohen, AR	0.359	0.239	0.419	0.209	0.347	0.039	0.032	0.278	0.325	0.398	0.441	0.213	0.294
Conger, JA	0.437	0.363	0.522	0.219	0.294	0.053	0.106	0.354	0.397	0.418	0.507	0.249	0.324

Appendix C (Cont.)

Co-citation Correlation Matrix

	Adler, NJ	Alvesson, M	Argyris, C	Armenakis, AA	Bandura, A	Barr, PS	Bartlett, CA	Bartunek, J	Beckhard, R	Bedeian, A	Beer, M	Beer, S	Benne, KD
Cooperrider, D	0.267	0.531	0.653	0.111	0.051	0.190	0.107	0.579	0.446	0.180	0.497	0.483	0.340
Cummings, TG	0.330	0.336	0.618	0.227	0.132	0.057	0.055	0.418	0.532	0.395	0.721	0.373	0.380
Daft, RL	0.422	0.527	0.628	0.109	0.076	0.454	0.338	0.706	0.163	0.291	0.332	0.505	0.177
Davis, DA	-0.010	-0.034	0.020	-0.005	0.618	-0.046	-0.066	-0.030	-0.019	0.023	-0.014	-0.037	-0.005
DiClemente, CC	-0.044	-0.073	-0.060	-0.014	0.864	-0.061	-0.061	-0.073	-0.071	-0.020	-0.077	-0.071	-0.040
DiMaggio, P	0.314	0.328	0.231	-0.014	0.006	0.232	0.263	0.281	0.017	0.057	0.121	0.164	-0.017
Dunphy, D	0.428	0.457	0.647	0.235	0.143	0.142	0.143	0.490	0.565	0.330	0.718	0.386	0.471
Eddy, W	0.093	0.086	0.361	0.130	0.109	-0.034	-0.044	0.233	0.516	0.196	0.420	0.187	0.357
Ford, JD	0.342	0.567	0.569	0.160	0.123	0.483	0.224	0.678	0.198	0.302	0.357	0.441	0.189
French, JL	0.329	0.254	0.392	0.083	0.124	0.181	0.184	0.338	0.118	0.289	0.309	0.231	0.114
French, W	0.214	0.319	0.658	0.186	0.090	0.014	0.010	0.367	0.847	0.222	0.793	0.401	0.616
Galbraith, JR	0.428	0.338	0.506	0.067	0.023	0.272	0.396	0.464	0.193	0.234	0.329	0.426	0.159
Ghoshal, S	0.669	0.306	0.319	-0.002	-0.008	0.211	0.968	0.278	0.038	0.126	0.186	0.225	-0.006
Golembiewski, RT	0.286	0.339	0.662	0.522	0.171	0.051	0.002	0.488	0.645	0.615	0.692	0.405	0.516
Goodstein, LD	0.268	0.262	0.503	0.176	0.104	-0.035	0.005	0.251	0.636	0.235	0.566	0.249	0.473
Gray, B	0.502	0.556	0.537	0.082	0.034	0.350	0.345	0.639	0.184	0.229	0.344	0.376	0.196
Greenwood, R	0.319	0.534	0.426	0.047	0.056	0.376	0.254	0.607	0.121	0.134	0.262	0.356	0.087
Greiner, L	0.339	0.451	0.662	0.151	0.034	0.285	0.221	0.587	0.500	0.262	0.530	0.483	0.363
Greve, MS	0.045	0.009	0.061	-0.013	-0.032	-0.036	0.059	-0.024	0.074	-0.022	0.083	0.010	0.013
Harris, RT	0.183	0.197	0.525	0.138	0.175	-0.019	0.000	0.211	0.558	0.210	0.442	0.313	0.382
Harrison, Roger	0.278	0.455	0.667	0.203	0.129	0.059	0.032	0.420	0.698	0.280	0.647	0.465	0.506
Heneman, RL	0.155	0.073	0.186	0.245	0.089	-0.025	-0.003	0.067	0.114	0.437	0.348	0.058	0.064
Hersey, P	0.202	0.214	0.437	0.132	0.142	-0.022	-0.006	0.240	0.435	0.186	0.370	0.248	0.514

87

Appendix C (Cont.)

Co-citation Correlation Matrix

	Adler, NJ	Alvesson, M	Argyris, C	Armenakis, AA	Bandura, A	Barr, PS	Bartlett, CA	Bartunek, J	Beckhard, R	Bedeian, A	Beer, M	Beer, S	Benne, KD
Hirschhorn, L	0.395	0.562	0.761	0.133	0.101	0.206	0.179	0.527	0.447	0.280	0.564	0.562	0.351
Hornstein, H	0.285	0.176	0.475	0.170	0.380	-0.056	-0.003	0.233	0.531	0.310	0.505	0.216	0.503
Hough, JR	0.088	0.153	0.156	-0.041	-0.032	0.165	0.117	0.231	-0.076	0.057	-0.009	0.117	-0.064
Huff, AS	0.239	0.447	0.476	0.060	0.013	0.826	0.243	0.616	0.088	0.148	0.232	0.381	0.070
Huy, QN	0.370	0.487	0.506	0.283	0.120	0.266	0.184	0.622	0.298	0.408	0.496	0.300	0.214
Jensen, MC	0.330	0.174	0.227	-0.027	0.005	0.214	0.332	0.194	-0.016	0.139	0.130	0.137	-0.030
Kakabadse, A	0.277	0.386	0.601	0.146	0.034	0.081	0.105	0.427	0.543	0.222	0.601	0.380	0.378
Kanter, RM	0.686	0.629	0.790	0.260	0.178	0.248	0.332	0.594	0.466	0.524	0.690	0.505	0.380
Kiesler, S	0.284	0.289	0.399	0.056	0.139	0.331	0.181	0.480	0.049	0.209	0.163	0.270	0.140
Kim, WC	0.385	0.121	0.136	0.004	-0.029	0.109	0.581	0.103	-0.036	0.038	0.049	0.084	-0.060
Kotter, J	0.518	0.564	0.751	0.279	0.125	0.177	0.235	0.542	0.588	0.423	0.750	0.466	0.403
Langley, A	0.239	0.508	0.365	0.032	-0.019	0.364	0.229	0.552	0.072	0.109	0.220	0.320	0.043
Lawler, EE	0.500	0.379	0.678	0.291	0.281	0.081	0.137	0.416	0.464	0.586	0.723	0.398	0.394
Lawrence, PR	0.486	0.460	0.647	0.112	0.035	0.309	0.390	0.558	0.308	0.285	0.424	0.525	0.258
Ledford, GE	0.311	0.223	0.410	0.145	0.168	0.013	0.050	0.279	0.281	0.374	0.522	0.205	0.228
Lewin, K	0.341	0.372	0.669	0.257	0.552	0.103	0.047	0.433	0.517	0.390	0.543	0.417	0.600
Lorsch, JW	0.266	0.163	0.286	0.014	-0.007	0.180	0.188	0.229	0.147	0.149	0.209	0.193	0.087
Mathews, J	0.314	0.221	0.424	0.028	0.223	0.058	0.311	0.200	0.152	0.175	0.404	0.316	0.103
Mauborgne, R	0.191	0.060	0.080	0.071	-0.015	0.018	0.308	0.048	-0.009	0.090	0.039	0.051	-0.034
Miller, RH	-0.036	-0.012	0.009	-0.024	0.183	-0.011	-0.042	-0.016	-0.058	-0.006	-0.035	-0.021	-0.026
Mirvis, P	0.428	0.377	0.579	0.267	0.158	0.048	0.119	0.380	0.455	0.498	0.646	0.320	0.374
Moore, L	0.057	-0.006	0.007	0.013	0.729	-0.050	-0.054	-0.028	-0.039	0.059	-0.024	-0.049	0.004
Morrison, EW	0.393	0.333	0.436	0.227	0.246	0.076	0.129	0.308	0.203	0.528	0.342	0.218	0.176

Appendix C (Cont.)

Co-citation Correlation Matrix

	Adler, NJ	Alvesson, M	Argyris, C	Armenakis, AA	Bandura, A	Barr, PS	Bartlett, CA	Bartunek, J	Beckhard, R	Bedeian, A	Beer, M	Beer, S	Berne, KD
Mouton, JS	0.165	0.084	0.187	0.004	0.051	-0.018	0.053	0.109	0.178	0.074	0.122	0.101	0.325
Nelson, RR	0.281	0.316	0.436	0.000	0.043	0.308	0.366	0.370	0.048	0.098	0.175	0.326	0.025
Nohria, N	0.558	0.319	0.308	-0.018	-0.022	0.223	0.799	0.269	0.020	0.091	0.195	0.207	-0.011
O'Reilly, C	0.648	0.443	0.564	0.276	0.221	0.244	0.309	0.481	0.241	0.610	0.486	0.299	0.231
Palmer, I	0.166	0.782	0.346	0.054	-0.009	0.180	0.085	0.406	0.084	0.098	0.207	0.313	0.063
Pasmore, WA	0.298	0.371	0.596	0.259	0.115	0.047	0.034	0.456	0.488	0.376	0.664	0.385	0.387
Pettigrew, AM	0.438	0.739	0.718	0.157	0.038	0.406	0.300	0.728	0.376	0.292	0.547	0.545	0.273
Poole, MS	0.329	0.437	0.456	0.110	0.062	0.352	0.183	0.538	0.118	0.225	0.242	0.339	0.259
Porras, JI	0.223	0.264	0.581	0.377	0.163	0.068	0.010	0.453	0.700	0.399	0.791	0.320	0.453
Potter, J	0.214	0.708	0.310	0.058	0.291	0.121	0.068	0.381	0.081	0.125	0.171	0.254	0.124
Powell, WW	0.340	0.338	0.258	-0.014	0.003	0.246	0.310	0.298	0.019	0.069	0.132	0.186	-0.009
Prasad, P	0.337	0.721	0.523	0.060	0.035	0.231	0.171	0.548	0.210	0.169	0.301	0.391	0.215
Prochaska, JO	-0.036	-0.072	-0.055	-0.011	0.862	-0.061	-0.061	-0.069	-0.070	-0.011	-0.074	-0.071	-0.040
Quinn, RW	0.130	0.224	0.256	0.124	0.097	0.169	0.163	0.362	-0.025	0.233	0.127	0.206	-0.028
Rajagopalan, N	0.234	0.194	0.225	-0.014	-0.024	0.378	0.277	0.299	-0.029	0.108	0.097	0.147	-0.035
Reger, R	0.213	0.302	0.323	0.033	0.001	0.682	0.218	0.446	0.026	0.116	0.153	0.226	0.011
Romanelli, E	0.229	0.234	0.328	0.031	-0.005	0.325	0.230	0.408	0.098	0.125	0.205	0.203	0.049
Rousseau, D	0.513	0.429	0.528	0.304	0.198	0.135	0.205	0.400	0.246	0.639	0.442	0.275	0.226
Sashkin, M	0.342	0.296	0.545	0.212	0.146	0.000	0.048	0.312	0.555	0.340	0.606	0.266	0.403
Schaffer, RH	0.280	0.336	0.610	0.148	0.096	0.088	0.147	0.337	0.485	0.255	0.762	0.392	0.279
Schein, E	0.558	0.680	0.926	0.271	0.184	0.226	0.215	0.662	0.656	0.488	0.770	0.618	0.522
Sebastian, JG	-0.011	0.058	-0.011	-0.032	-0.031	0.048	0.002	0.111	-0.055	-0.037	-0.035	0.036	-0.038
Senge, PM	0.304	0.490	0.872	0.136	0.102	0.269	0.206	0.550	0.425	0.232	0.583	0.714	0.302

Co-citation Correlation Matrix

	Adler, NJ	Alvesson, M	Argyris, C	Armenakis, AA	Bandura, A	Barr, PS	Bartlett, CA	Bartunek, J	Beckhard, R	Bedeian, A	Beer, M	Beer, S	Benne, KD
Shani, R	0.154	0.194	0.344	0.003	-0.020	0.086	0.054	0.255	0.246	0.078	0.373	0.229	0.128
Shortell, SM	0.277	0.273	0.274	0.032	0.042	0.266	0.207	0.287	0.006	0.214	0.143	0.160	0.007
Sproull, LS	0.102	0.171	0.213	0.025	0.035	0.167	0.048	0.269	0.018	0.083	0.062	0.142	0.057
Stacey, RD	0.245	0.564	0.692	0.093	0.020	0.344	0.206	0.553	0.275	0.170	0.427	0.652	0.202
Stevenson, WB	0.544	0.426	0.470	0.122	0.065	0.203	0.394	0.459	0.164	0.351	0.405	0.292	0.134
Stewart, WH	0.368	0.322	0.429	0.048	0.219	0.226	0.298	0.393	0.114	0.228	0.211	0.391	0.119
Stimpert, JL	0.144	0.183	0.248	0.013	0.098	0.925	0.175	0.339	-0.033	0.074	0.072	0.157	-0.030
Tannenbaum, R	0.208	0.227	0.510	0.135	0.125	-0.019	-0.001	0.278	0.552	0.198	0.480	0.288	0.539
Tsoukas, H	0.274	0.793	0.549	0.069	0.016	0.331	0.271	0.611	0.136	0.153	0.277	0.602	0.108
Tushman, M	0.430	0.432	0.564	0.076	0.030	0.413	0.398	0.578	0.166	0.249	0.336	0.413	0.135
Van de Ven, AH	0.493	0.509	0.580	0.107	0.040	0.411	0.430	0.591	0.161	0.281	0.343	0.434	0.182
van Dick, R	0.162	0.121	0.185	0.119	0.303	-0.004	-0.021	0.118	0.072	0.321	0.117	0.083	0.147
Walton, RE	0.440	0.356	0.663	0.175	0.128	0.081	0.137	0.450	0.571	0.382	0.730	0.402	0.498
Weick, KE	0.515	0.690	0.787	0.152	0.116	0.467	0.353	0.777	0.300	0.362	0.486	0.606	0.266
White, MC	0.372	0.269	0.341	0.194	0.154	0.225	0.140	0.305	0.132	0.357	0.275	0.177	0.092
Winter, SG	0.150	0.181	0.283	-0.033	-0.006	0.173	0.295	0.184	-0.009	0.021	0.066	0.212	-0.028
Woodman, R	0.442	0.470	0.646	0.352	0.194	0.216	0.173	0.571	0.452	0.527	0.702	0.376	0.349
Wruck, KH	0.023	-0.044	-0.013	-0.053	-0.027	0.023	0.045	-0.024	-0.061	-0.016	-0.020	-0.012	-0.065
Zajac, EJ	0.310	0.230	0.229	-0.024	-0.015	0.373	0.340	0.289	-0.046	0.106	0.094	0.140	-0.042

Appendix C (Cont.)

Co-citation Correlation Matrix

	Bennis, W	Blake, RR	Boeker, W	Bower, JL	Brown, LD	Burke, WW	Bushe, G	Coch, L	Cohen, AR	Conger, JA	Coopeider, D	Cummings, TG	Daft, RL
Adler, NJ													
Alvesson, M													
Argyris, C													
Armenakis, AA													
Bandura, A													
Barr, PS													
Bartlett, CA													
Bartunek, J													
Beckhard, R													
Bedeian, A													
Beer, M													
Beer, S													
Benne, KD													
Bennis, W	1.000												
Blake, RR	0.678	1.000											
Boeker, W	0.065	-0.034	1.000										
Bower, JL	0.242	0.100	0.518	1.000									
Brown, LD	0.392	0.529	0.214	0.224	1.000								
Burke, WW	0.710	0.590	-0.086	0.058	0.315	1.000							
Bushe, G	0.563	0.404	0.020	0.183	0.260	0.591	1.000						
Coch, L	0.593	0.530	-0.010	0.132	0.351	0.584	0.497	1.000					
Cohen, AR	0.537	0.357	0.118	0.161	0.216	0.343	0.353	0.371	1.000				
Conger, JA	0.766	0.441	0.109	0.180	0.204	0.457	0.463	0.418	0.605	1.000			

Appendix C (Cont.)

Co-citation Correlation Matrix

	Bennis, W	Blake, RR	Boeker, W	Bower, JL	Brown, LD	Burke, WW	Bushe, G	Coch, L	Cohen, AR	Conger, JA	Cooperrider, D	Cummings, TG	Daft, RL
Cooperrider, D	0.524	0.336	0.034	0.191	0.515	0.416	0.503	0.402	0.236	0.309	1.000		
Cummings, TG	0.555	0.497	0.039	0.210	0.373	0.599	0.661	0.565	0.409	0.471	0.427	1.000	
Daft, RL	0.335	0.180	0.410	0.661	0.295	0.104	0.286	0.193	0.221	0.264	0.336	0.328	1.000
Davis, DA	0.006	0.001	-0.029	-0.066	0.065	-0.024	-0.052	0.007	0.128	0.101	-0.039	-0.020	-0.024
DiClemente, CC	-0.056	-0.046	-0.073	-0.078	-0.071	-0.068	-0.065	-0.033	0.061	0.016	-0.068	-0.058	-0.064
DiMaggio, P	0.082	-0.007	0.499	0.344	0.236	-0.034	0.031	0.006	0.021	0.077	0.118	0.078	0.356
Dunphy, D	0.713	0.388	0.156	0.277	0.279	0.545	0.478	0.516	0.417	0.534	0.442	0.597	0.318
Eddy, W	0.471	0.436	-0.068	0.041	0.183	0.495	0.282	0.266	0.285	0.267	0.251	0.372	0.115
Ford, JD	0.332	0.166	0.370	0.532	0.281	0.124	0.231	0.233	0.256	0.261	0.408	0.316	0.762
French, JL	0.285	0.130	0.264	0.430	0.209	0.158	0.364	0.209	0.287	0.328	0.172	0.379	0.539
French, W	0.736	0.642	-0.054	0.096	0.398	0.856	0.539	0.578	0.354	0.378	0.488	0.621	0.173
Galbraith, JR	0.311	0.223	0.412	0.709	0.297	0.135	0.303	0.199	0.228	0.228	0.214	0.346	0.784
Ghoshal, S	0.137	0.020	0.354	0.529	0.144	-0.015	0.098	0.021	0.060	0.140	0.153	0.098	0.455
Golembiewski, RT	0.663	0.571	-0.011	0.120	0.389	0.703	0.545	0.538	0.486	0.492	0.498	0.626	0.264
Goodstein, LD	0.630	0.511	-0.079	0.055	0.207	0.821	0.447	0.402	0.317	0.397	0.349	0.448	0.123
Gray, B	0.350	0.215	0.409	0.484	0.650	0.156	0.251	0.171	0.190	0.284	0.484	0.319	0.639
Greenwood, R	0.232	0.069	0.497	0.515	0.266	0.057	0.129	0.090	0.101	0.193	0.261	0.172	0.562
Greiner, L	0.576	0.406	0.471	0.587	0.386	0.398	0.386	0.408	0.339	0.356	0.412	0.424	0.589
Greve, MS	0.146	0.014	0.164	0.079	0.127	0.045	0.017	0.021	0.032	0.109	-0.016	-0.014	-0.012
Harris, RT	0.537	0.420	-0.048	0.081	0.227	0.458	0.394	0.563	0.325	0.330	0.339	0.473	0.081
Harrison, Roger	0.721	0.571	0.003	0.144	0.330	0.627	0.466	0.445	0.335	0.454	0.489	0.433	0.228
Heneman, RL	0.158	0.095	0.020	0.031	0.047	0.214	0.421	0.265	0.218	0.304	0.059	0.428	0.095
Hersey, P	0.629	0.824	-0.040	0.057	0.298	0.419	0.218	0.398	0.294	0.553	0.233	0.275	0.111

Appendix C (Cont.)

Co-citation Correlation Matrix

	Bennis, W	Blake, RR	Boeker, W	Bower, JL	Brown, LD	Burke, WW	Bushe, G	Coch, L	Cohen, AR	Conger, JA	Cooperrider, D	Cummings, TG	Daft, RL
Hirschhorn, L	0.642	0.425	0.142	0.359	0.372	0.390	0.458	0.385	0.393	0.457	0.509	0.530	0.484
Hornstein, H	0.613	0.627	-0.068	0.018	0.320	0.567	0.383	0.512	0.539	0.569	0.287	0.459	0.101
Hough, JR	-0.016	-0.096	0.222	0.428	0.012	-0.115	-0.031	-0.049	-0.066	-0.006	-0.027	0.021	0.481
Huff, AS	0.197	0.051	0.459	0.556	0.186	0.019	0.147	0.120	0.105	0.139	0.296	0.153	0.654
Huy, QN	0.434	0.206	0.255	0.392	0.191	0.277	0.279	0.290	0.406	0.418	0.375	0.331	0.435
Jensen, MC	0.063	0.002	0.744	0.472	0.296	-0.069	0.069	0.020	0.119	0.127	0.024	0.093	0.358
Kakabadse, A	0.632	0.418	0.125	0.263	0.345	0.500	0.369	0.392	0.357	0.402	0.420	0.393	0.217
Kanter, RM	0.719	0.464	0.390	0.557	0.439	0.463	0.567	0.453	0.593	0.658	0.470	0.601	0.637
Kiesler, S	0.198	0.109	0.254	0.380	0.156	0.009	0.150	0.127	0.188	0.183	0.165	0.176	0.780
Kim, WC	0.020	-0.045	0.264	0.325	0.086	-0.094	0.004	-0.047	0.012	0.043	0.041	0.011	0.222
Kotter, J	0.832	0.481	0.239	0.409	0.318	0.587	0.520	0.495	0.549	0.714	0.466	0.548	0.467
Langley, A	0.171	0.008	0.406	0.573	0.182	0.021	0.103	0.041	0.060	0.146	0.231	0.150	0.586
Lawler, EE	0.622	0.524	0.168	0.279	0.410	0.529	0.682	0.595	0.598	0.670	0.388	0.800	0.409
Lawrence, PR	0.444	0.387	0.452	0.713	0.411	0.232	0.377	0.299	0.298	0.291	0.332	0.419	0.798
Ledford, GE	0.366	0.302	0.063	0.125	0.229	0.352	0.621	0.425	0.368	0.482	0.242	0.769	0.236
Lewin, K	0.637	0.556	0.047	0.165	0.421	0.504	0.396	0.712	0.555	0.541	0.448	0.496	0.280
Lorsch, JW	0.217	0.158	0.640	0.418	0.296	0.077	0.163	0.133	0.189	0.191	0.088	0.152	0.336
Mathews, J	0.249	0.148	0.197	0.305	0.284	0.197	0.321	0.275	0.205	0.265	0.183	0.442	0.341
Mauborgne, R	0.025	-0.019	0.080	0.150	0.010	-0.047	0.016	-0.017	0.035	0.042	0.023	0.023	0.103
Miller, RH	-0.022	-0.014	0.066	-0.007	0.331	-0.060	-0.060	-0.039	-0.004	-0.001	-0.004	-0.043	0.029
Mirvis, P	0.536	0.461	0.057	0.164	0.326	0.547	0.645	0.496	0.459	0.524	0.417	0.639	0.294
Moore, L	0.002	-0.007	-0.069	-0.070	-0.001	-0.041	-0.039	0.035	0.166	0.104	-0.039	-0.007	-0.017
Morrison, EW	0.327	0.212	0.137	0.150	0.199	0.199	0.279	0.232	0.364	0.433	0.255	0.338	0.276

93

Appendix C (Cont.)

Co-citation Correlation Matrix

	Bennis, W	Blake, RR	Boeker, W	Bower, JL	Brown, LD	Burke, WW	Bushe, G	Coch, L	Cohen, AR	Conger, JA	Cooperrider, D	Cummings, TG	Daft, RL
Mouton, JS	0.216	0.615	-0.012	0.033	0.253	0.138	0.044	0.161	0.112	0.154	0.061	0.098	0.069
Nelson, RR	0.142	0.035	0.548	0.714	0.212	-0.012	0.094	0.086	0.096	0.111	0.148	0.139	0.568
Nohria, N	0.111	-0.001	0.438	0.504	0.187	-0.018	0.083	0.018	0.033	0.098	0.142	0.103	0.460
O'Reilly, C	0.446	0.282	0.543	0.506	0.331	0.247	0.443	0.298	0.555	0.545	0.263	0.463	0.613
Palmer, I	0.202	0.066	0.121	0.204	0.203	0.070	0.081	0.073	0.093	0.165	0.372	0.128	0.341
Pasmore, WA	0.548	0.485	-0.006	0.180	0.440	0.613	0.664	0.564	0.413	0.469	0.620	0.825	0.337
Pettigrew, AM	0.534	0.285	0.467	0.687	0.344	0.305	0.360	0.291	0.292	0.387	0.452	0.404	0.704
Poole, MS	0.254	0.142	0.282	0.426	0.219	0.072	0.185	0.135	0.140	0.179	0.282	0.234	0.757
Porras, JI	0.602	0.510	-0.034	0.108	0.333	0.840	0.540	0.540	0.397	0.388	0.457	0.614	0.230
Potter, J	0.213	0.096	0.042	0.123	0.182	0.060	0.059	0.190	0.210	0.247	0.326	0.117	0.281
Powell, WW	0.089	-0.004	0.525	0.392	0.255	-0.033	0.038	0.010	0.021	0.084	0.131	0.085	0.394
Prasad, P	0.341	0.172	0.230	0.316	0.292	0.144	0.192	0.170	0.161	0.231	0.444	0.227	0.532
Prochaska, JO	-0.052	-0.041	-0.073	-0.078	-0.069	-0.065	-0.064	-0.026	0.081	0.032	-0.067	-0.053	-0.062
Quinn, RW	0.078	-0.024	0.172	0.280	0.131	-0.009	0.118	0.057	0.097	0.169	0.096	0.146	0.439
Rajagopalan, N	0.037	-0.058	0.767	0.500	0.203	-0.099	0.031	-0.014	0.064	0.065	0.054	0.056	0.474
Reger, R	0.111	-0.007	0.472	0.457	0.137	-0.027	0.118	0.053	0.069	0.106	0.167	0.090	0.513
Romanelli, E	0.172	0.033	0.707	0.635	0.161	0.019	0.113	0.094	0.149	0.159	0.125	0.152	0.511
Rousseau, D	0.418	0.286	0.247	0.274	0.297	0.271	0.424	0.297	0.417	0.526	0.292	0.485	0.439
Sashkin, M	0.790	0.566	0.008	0.133	0.246	0.709	0.542	0.533	0.447	0.848	0.343	0.513	0.196
Schaffer, RH	0.536	0.328	0.124	0.272	0.232	0.523	0.485	0.451	0.341	0.399	0.341	0.502	0.305
Schein, E	0.827	0.576	0.223	0.404	0.449	0.609	0.587	0.565	0.520	0.627	0.622	0.620	0.540
Sebastian, JG	-0.038	-0.057	0.069	0.019	0.009	-0.063	-0.058	-0.057	-0.073	-0.026	-0.029	-0.060	0.020
Senge, PM	0.562	0.350	0.149	0.369	0.334	0.413	0.389	0.360	0.272	0.377	0.541	0.441	0.498

Appendix C (Cont.)

Co-citation Correlation Matrix

	Bennis, W	Blake, RR	Boeker, W	Bower, JL	Brown, LD	Burke, WW	Bushe, G	Coch, L	Cohen, AR	Conger, JA	Cooperrider, D	Cummings, TG	Daft, RL
Shani, R	0.273	0.193	0.063	0.165	0.132	0.210	0.477	0.212	0.117	0.201	0.173	0.328	0.267
Shortell, SM	0.116	0.034	0.573	0.369	0.362	-0.017	0.097	0.030	0.099	0.169	0.116	0.143	0.447
Sproull, LS	0.097	0.050	0.088	0.173	0.067	-0.013	0.086	0.054	0.071	0.063	0.088	0.085	0.438
Stacey, RD	0.396	0.199	0.278	0.477	0.273	0.229	0.258	0.251	0.161	0.223	0.447	0.326	0.594
Stevenson, WB	0.350	0.216	0.497	0.532	0.300	0.155	0.368	0.250	0.367	0.399	0.218	0.391	0.621
Stewart, WH	0.257	0.148	0.383	0.462	0.254	0.047	0.138	0.108	0.262	0.281	0.182	0.183	0.616
Stimpert, JL	0.043	-0.038	0.427	0.358	0.076	-0.090	0.016	0.022	0.089	0.089	0.112	0.023	0.397
Tannenbaum, R	0.647	0.785	-0.064	0.075	0.310	0.530	0.329	0.561	0.324	0.464	0.308	0.408	0.119
Tsoukas, H	0.260	0.092	0.262	0.457	0.215	0.076	0.171	0.123	0.119	0.176	0.401	0.213	0.644
Tushman, M	0.309	0.142	0.675	0.837	0.289	0.093	0.241	0.177	0.239	0.252	0.244	0.292	0.807
Van de Ven, AH	0.321	0.172	0.551	0.732	0.352	0.106	0.273	0.182	0.210	0.258	0.313	0.338	0.823
van Dick, R	0.156	0.139	0.000	-0.002	0.129	0.099	0.087	0.182	0.260	0.262	0.061	0.146	0.152
Walton, RE	0.630	0.733	0.115	0.300	0.540	0.582	0.662	0.542	0.473	0.506	0.396	0.822	0.419
Weick, KE	0.493	0.295	0.468	0.696	0.395	0.234	0.377	0.308	0.323	0.388	0.459	0.431	0.932
White, MC	0.331	0.175	0.486	0.420	0.152	0.110	0.206	0.137	0.417	0.382	0.099	0.213	0.425
Winter, SG	0.038	-0.022	0.348	0.523	0.093	-0.053	0.009	0.018	0.006	0.009	0.055	0.038	0.338
Woodman, R	0.577	0.391	0.212	0.400	0.355	0.569	0.568	0.445	0.477	0.531	0.440	0.596	0.503
Wruck, KH	-0.047	-0.054	0.354	0.127	0.193	-0.089	-0.025	-0.047	-0.026	-0.001	-0.071	-0.047	0.042
Zajac, EJ	0.041	-0.044	0.863	0.517	0.307	-0.105	0.032	-0.022	0.076	0.093	0.051	0.052	0.477

Co-citation Correlation Matrix

	DiClemente, CC	DiMaggio, P	Dunphy, D	Eddy, W	Ford, JD	French, JL	French, W	Galbraith, JR	Ghoshal, S	Golembiewski, RT	Goodstein, LD	Gray, B	Greenwood, R
Cooperrider, D													
Cummings, TG													
Daft, RL													
Davis, DA													
DiClemente, CC	1.000												
DiMaggio, P	-0.044	1.000											
Dunphy, D	-0.052	0.108	1.000										
Eddy, W	-0.012	-0.044	0.270	1.000									
Ford, JD	-0.031	0.301	0.390	0.111	1.000								
French, JL	-0.014	0.145	0.308	0.067	0.433	1.000							
French, W	-0.060	0.011	0.569	0.523	0.189	0.118	1.000						
Galbraith, JR	-0.069	0.299	0.292	0.111	0.588	0.522	0.168	1.000					
Ghoshal, S	-0.071	0.377	0.175	-0.031	0.328	0.256	0.022	0.467	1.000				
Golembiewski, RT	-0.040	0.027	0.527	0.649	0.280	0.213	0.691	0.195	0.045	1.000			
Goodstein, LD	-0.039	-0.030	0.432	0.470	0.114	0.130	0.691	0.098	0.005	0.581	1.000		
Gray, B	-0.084	0.549	0.339	0.066	0.625	0.431	0.195	0.521	0.462	0.267	0.125	1.000	
Greenwood, R	-0.033	0.701	0.351	0.031	0.569	0.283	0.099	0.448	0.372	0.131	0.036	0.650	1.000
Greiner, L	-0.087	0.281	0.537	0.284	0.582	0.454	0.439	0.642	0.305	0.418	0.347	0.546	0.493
Greve, MS	-0.036	0.013	0.074	-0.007	-0.027	0.042	0.042	0.018	0.090	-0.021	0.034	0.002	0.008
Harris, RT	-0.001	-0.017	0.366	0.394	0.100	0.139	0.514	0.119	0.009	0.555	0.402	0.086	0.020
Harrison, Roger	-0.024	0.044	0.517	0.406	0.247	0.168	0.740	0.178	0.061	0.628	0.565	0.267	0.190
Heneman, RL	-0.031	0.023	0.182	0.083	0.074	0.264	0.146	0.105	0.025	0.310	0.128	0.058	0.011
Hersey, P	-0.007	-0.021	0.340	0.273	0.108	0.086	0.433	0.092	0.000	0.395	0.394	0.110	0.052

Appendix C (Cont.)

Co-citation Correlation Matrix

	Diclemente, CC	DiMaggio, P	Dunphy, D	Eddy, W	Ford, JD	French, JL	French, W	Galbraith, JR	Ghoshal, S	Golembiewski, RT	Goodstein, LD	Gray, B	Greenwood, R
Hirschhorn, L	-0.049	0.205	0.530	0.268	0.453	0.348	0.443	0.399	0.244	0.497	0.368	0.459	0.324
Hornstein, H	0.059	-0.047	0.411	0.406	0.133	0.185	0.572	0.087	0.004	0.560	0.549	0.134	0.006
Hough, JR	-0.053	0.273	0.018	-0.071	0.280	0.260	-0.080	0.394	0.186	-0.062	-0.092	0.249	0.289
Huff, AS	-0.078	0.360	0.253	-0.002	0.659	0.280	0.096	0.435	0.344	0.141	0.015	0.523	0.554
Huy, QN	-0.059	0.146	0.563	0.089	0.583	0.330	0.265	0.337	0.243	0.351	0.213	0.422	0.456
Jensen, MC	-0.075	0.479	0.082	-0.054	0.263	0.249	-0.039	0.393	0.440	0.015	-0.071	0.378	0.409
Kakabadse, A	-0.085	0.132	0.539	0.269	0.224	0.206	0.584	0.233	0.138	0.469	0.384	0.329	0.246
Kanter, RM	-0.059	0.372	0.655	0.256	0.577	0.581	0.455	0.612	0.428	0.556	0.416	0.660	0.506
Kiesler, S	-0.015	0.214	0.178	0.091	0.528	0.387	0.063	0.457	0.267	0.156	0.072	0.383	0.348
Kim, WC	-0.064	0.227	0.051	-0.077	0.151	0.125	-0.069	0.246	0.609	-0.045	-0.062	0.307	0.198
Kotter, J	-0.060	0.164	0.715	0.267	0.466	0.397	0.566	0.439	0.287	0.536	0.483	0.454	0.362
Langley, A	-0.080	0.398	0.331	-0.026	0.560	0.314	0.062	0.461	0.326	0.071	-0.007	0.557	0.710
Lawler, EE	-0.019	0.135	0.565	0.341	0.360	0.467	0.508	0.431	0.206	0.668	0.419	0.365	0.213
Lawrence, PR	-0.082	0.411	0.362	0.202	0.658	0.488	0.290	0.938	0.482	0.317	0.184	0.618	0.534
Ledford, GE	-0.028	0.072	0.514	0.206	0.201	0.326	0.308	0.249	0.088	0.478	0.255	0.224	0.125
Lewin, K	0.150	0.066	0.582	0.325	0.351	0.246	0.577	0.197	0.084	0.566	0.456	0.269	0.203
Lorsch, JW	-0.069	0.205	0.164	0.068	0.289	0.231	0.104	0.469	0.261	0.115	0.050	0.275	0.261
Mathews, J	0.075	0.318	0.324	0.081	0.240	0.390	0.223	0.430	0.360	0.209	0.103	0.328	0.273
Mauborgne, R	-0.043	0.027	0.032	-0.037	0.060	0.048	-0.038	0.107	0.317	0.008	-0.029	0.131	0.045
Miller, RH	0.165	0.046	-0.053	-0.041	0.010	0.032	-0.016	0.041	-0.021	-0.028	-0.065	0.179	0.039
Mirvis, P	-0.045	0.112	0.465	0.319	0.255	0.351	0.495	0.258	0.168	0.654	0.456	0.300	0.179
Moore, L	0.698	-0.027	0.018	0.003	0.020	0.033	-0.024	-0.049	-0.061	0.015	-0.002	-0.023	-0.013
Morrison, EW	0.018	0.110	0.303	0.182	0.275	0.260	0.218	0.178	0.203	0.444	0.218	0.284	0.159

Co-citation Correlation Matrix

	DiClemente, CC	DiMaggio, P	Dunphy, D	Eddy, W	Ford, JD	French, JL	French, W	Galbraith, JR	Ghoshal, S	Golembiewski, RT	Goodstein, LD	Gray, B	Greenwood, R
Mouton, JS	-0.032	0.052	0.079	0.163	0.051	0.037	0.170	0.062	0.060	0.197	0.168	0.098	0.080
Nelson, RR	-0.050	0.500	0.165	-0.015	0.422	0.326	0.041	0.526	0.488	0.065	-0.003	0.437	0.504
Nohria, N	-0.072	0.584	0.161	-0.048	0.350	0.276	0.008	0.469	0.876	0.022	-0.021	0.570	0.477
O'Reilly, C	-0.033	0.306	0.453	0.163	0.524	0.552	0.224	0.549	0.416	0.444	0.252	0.531	0.421
Palmer, I	-0.064	0.213	0.236	-0.032	0.524	0.120	0.108	0.183	0.155	0.117	0.066	0.426	0.383
Pasmore, WA	-0.068	0.032	0.524	0.356	0.309	0.338	0.557	0.327	0.071	0.643	0.431	0.340	0.162
Pettigrew, AM	-0.092	0.394	0.610	0.134	0.683	0.425	0.363	0.607	0.408	0.360	0.253	0.657	0.722
Poole, MS	-0.053	0.267	0.328	0.078	0.653	0.439	0.106	0.501	0.289	0.199	0.126	0.541	0.489
Porras, JI	-0.013	0.024	0.545	0.530	0.259	0.204	0.792	0.187	0.030	0.816	0.636	0.214	0.149
Potter, J	0.115	0.208	0.258	0.035	0.397	0.102	0.119	0.112	0.119	0.146	0.090	0.335	0.461
Powell, WW	-0.051	0.933	0.121	-0.044	0.336	0.191	0.010	0.345	0.418	0.026	-0.024	0.568	0.715
Prasad, P	-0.067	0.469	0.330	0.075	0.467	0.203	0.227	0.332	0.262	0.275	0.187	0.504	0.549
Prochaska, JO	0.939	-0.044	-0.046	-0.002	-0.027	-0.008	-0.057	-0.068	-0.071	-0.032	-0.029	-0.084	-0.035
Quinn, RW	-0.016	0.084	0.104	-0.013	0.330	0.259	-0.013	0.261	0.215	0.105	-0.006	0.240	0.283
Rajagopalan, N	-0.084	0.334	0.135	-0.069	0.403	0.285	-0.056	0.447	0.390	-0.013	-0.072	0.418	0.414
Reger, R	-0.069	0.377	0.151	-0.040	0.522	0.252	0.023	0.362	0.310	0.061	-0.027	0.450	0.453
Romanelli, E	-0.062	0.372	0.327	-0.018	0.474	0.397	0.040	0.544	0.320	0.063	0.015	0.409	0.523
Rousseau, D	-0.031	0.193	0.398	0.199	0.411	0.420	0.255	0.365	0.302	0.508	0.260	0.452	0.276
Sashkin, M	-0.050	0.029	0.520	0.338	0.180	0.242	0.561	0.188	0.066	0.559	0.576	0.216	0.120
Schaffer, RH	-0.064	0.129	0.554	0.258	0.274	0.259	0.555	0.293	0.181	0.447	0.398	0.237	0.211
Schein, E	-0.055	0.211	0.704	0.367	0.523	0.388	0.666	0.436	0.295	0.697	0.558	0.526	0.406
Sebastian, JG	-0.031	0.177	0.024	-0.015	0.058	-0.023	-0.069	-0.006	0.037	-0.065	-0.088	0.151	0.576
Senge, PM	-0.036	0.165	0.472	0.231	0.412	0.273	0.481	0.348	0.278	0.486	0.366	0.388	0.297

Co-citation Correlation Matrix

	DiClemente, CC	DiMaggio, P	Dunphy, D	Eddy, W	Ford, JD	French, JL	French, W	Galbraith, JR	Ghoshal, S	Golembiewski, RT	Goodstein, LD	Gray, B	Greenwood, R
Shani, R	-0.079	0.195	0.231	0.067	0.185	0.156	0.285	0.244	0.088	0.191	0.130	0.198	0.166
Shortell, SM	-0.035	0.460	0.131	-0.021	0.366	0.301	0.017	0.427	0.333	0.094	-0.027	0.556	0.454
Sproull, LS	-0.034	0.103	0.059	0.054	0.275	0.157	0.027	0.199	0.100	0.074	0.022	0.192	0.174
Stacey, RD	-0.075	0.268	0.432	0.097	0.534	0.286	0.320	0.445	0.300	0.290	0.183	0.456	0.466
Stevenson, WB	-0.087	0.341	0.353	0.069	0.496	0.471	0.156	0.616	0.486	0.262	0.111	0.562	0.468
Stewart, WH	0.019	0.213	0.219	0.145	0.475	0.403	0.141	0.501	0.374	0.179	0.088	0.442	0.335
Stimpert, JL	-0.019	0.242	0.112	-0.033	0.451	0.192	-0.032	0.253	0.246	0.019	-0.061	0.316	0.353
Tannenbaum, R	-0.048	-0.010	0.398	0.384	0.119	0.107	0.553	0.117	0.004	0.497	0.486	0.108	0.044
Tsoukas, H	-0.069	0.335	0.290	0.022	0.607	0.253	0.159	0.410	0.379	0.197	0.088	0.518	0.536
Tushman, M	-0.085	0.487	0.377	0.059	0.670	0.547	0.131	0.818	0.523	0.184	0.077	0.629	0.650
Van de Ven, AH	-0.077	0.532	0.388	0.060	0.733	0.599	0.139	0.808	0.561	0.219	0.095	0.762	0.665
van Dick, R	0.111	-0.014	0.138	0.071	0.132	0.130	0.091	0.065	0.026	0.227	0.099	0.103	0.013
Walton, RE	-0.068	0.134	0.511	0.377	0.343	0.398	0.581	0.466	0.187	0.616	0.456	0.419	0.222
Weick, KE	-0.071	0.490	0.472	0.172	0.790	0.537	0.310	0.754	0.486	0.388	0.224	0.732	0.684
White, MC	-0.002	0.220	0.328	0.069	0.353	0.417	0.094	0.428	0.211	0.230	0.122	0.350	0.317
Winter, SG	-0.049	0.278	0.031	-0.044	0.204	0.146	-0.012	0.304	0.378	-0.011	-0.047	0.217	0.268
Woodman, R	-0.040	0.160	0.588	0.338	0.495	0.527	0.509	0.428	0.249	0.651	0.447	0.493	0.387
Wruck, KH	-0.032	0.049	-0.033	-0.067	0.013	0.090	-0.076	0.075	0.089	-0.075	-0.080	0.020	0.043
Zajac, EJ	-0.077	0.578	0.102	-0.082	0.388	0.307	-0.065	0.460	0.471	-0.020	-0.100	0.533	0.543

Appendix C (Cont.)

Co-citation Correlation Matrix

	Greiner, L	Greve, MS	Harris, RT	Harrison, Roger	Heneman, RL	Hersey, P	Hirschhorn, L	Hornstein, H	Hough, JR	Huff, AS	Huy, QN	Jensen, MC	Kakabadse, A
Cooperrider, D													
Cummings, TG													
Daft, RL													
Davis, DA													
DiClemente, CC													
DiMaggio, P													
Dunphy, D													
Eddy, W													
Ford, JD													
French, JL													
French, W													
Galbraith, JR													
Ghoshal, S													
Golembiewski, RT													
Goodstein, LD													
Gray, B													
Greenwood, R													
Greiner, L	1.000												
Greve, MS	0.041	1.000											
Harris, RT	0.271	0.050	1.000										
Harrison, Roger	0.459	0.039	0.560	1.000									
Heneman, RL	0.085	0.013	0.146	0.096	1.000								
Hersey, P	0.282	0.063	0.263	0.433	0.064	1.000							

Appendix C (Cont.)

Co-citation Correlation Matrix

	Greiner, L	Greve, MS	Harris, RT	Harrison, Roger	Heneman, RL	Hersey, P	Hirschhorn, L	Hornstein, H	Hough, JR	Huff, AS	Huy, QN	Jensen, MC	Kakabadse, A
Hirschhorn, L	0.491	0.049	0.376	0.508	0.144	0.314	1.000						
Hornstein, H	0.278	0.033	0.441	0.530	0.185	0.534	0.335	1.000					
Hough, JR	0.176	-0.023	-0.061	-0.054	-0.004	-0.082	0.093	-0.123	1.000				
Huff, AS	0.449	-0.021	0.020	0.161	0.008	0.033	0.344	-0.015	0.261	1.000			
Huy, QN	0.515	0.015	0.151	0.331	0.077	0.200	0.425	0.231	0.097	0.406	1.000		
Jensen, MC	0.310	0.341	0.012	0.005	0.149	-0.039	0.156	-0.013	0.203	0.315	0.128	1.000	
Kakabadse, A	0.521	0.084	0.379	0.615	0.093	0.317	0.492	0.347	0.055	0.210	0.370	0.123	1.000
Kanter, RM	0.690	0.083	0.372	0.535	0.282	0.369	0.705	0.447	0.179	0.422	0.620	0.399	0.556
Kiesler, S	0.333	-0.025	0.039	0.103	0.053	0.071	0.275	0.111	0.326	0.444	0.289	0.211	0.098
Kim, WC	0.146	0.073	-0.033	-0.035	-0.009	-0.052	0.092	-0.056	0.091	0.184	0.134	0.322	0.082
Kotter, J	0.615	0.244	0.366	0.569	0.196	0.480	0.638	0.450	0.073	0.331	0.635	0.224	0.589
Langley, A	0.490	-0.064	-0.061	0.156	-0.016	0.007	0.276	-0.053	0.412	0.545	0.504	0.262	0.248
Lawler, EE	0.455	0.074	0.443	0.469	0.605	0.348	0.578	0.573	0.048	0.196	0.399	0.311	0.420
Lawrence, PR	0.729	0.029	0.224	0.312	0.103	0.204	0.512	0.182	0.337	0.505	0.397	0.437	0.336
Ledford, GE	0.250	-0.017	0.297	0.237	0.598	0.169	0.377	0.353	0.008	0.083	0.226	0.150	0.216
Lewin, K	0.403	0.015	0.522	0.527	0.178	0.465	0.457	0.704	-0.022	0.211	0.408	0.058	0.420
Lorsch, JW	0.395	0.363	0.090	0.141	0.106	0.075	0.195	0.075	0.072	0.252	0.156	0.770	0.196
Mathews, J	0.271	0.241	0.218	0.144	0.327	0.068	0.381	0.218	0.149	0.159	0.088	0.415	0.195
Mauborgne, R	0.052	-0.001	-0.021	-0.011	0.004	-0.019	0.048	-0.023	0.002	0.058	0.113	0.117	0.064
Miller, RH	-0.001	-0.016	-0.021	-0.011	-0.035	-0.034	0.000	0.019	-0.043	-0.010	-0.059	0.051	-0.055
Mirvis, P	0.369	0.026	0.376	0.485	0.455	0.280	0.526	0.452	-0.012	0.139	0.344	0.179	0.366
Moore, L	-0.070	-0.051	0.051	0.014	0.003	0.015	-0.005	0.159	-0.046	-0.046	-0.001	-0.065	-0.047
Morrison, EW	0.214	0.042	0.215	0.291	0.294	0.161	0.318	0.353	0.078	0.147	0.388	0.193	0.225

Appendix C (Cont.)

Co-citation Correlation Matrix

	Greiner, L	Greve, MS	Harris, RT	Harrison, Roger	Heneman, RL	Hersey, P	Hirschhorn, L	Hornstein, H	Hough, JR	Huff, AS	Huy, QN	Jensen, MC	Kakabadse, A
Mouton, JS	0.095	-0.014	0.066	0.184	0.011	0.595	0.153	0.271	-0.045	0.014	0.033	0.034	0.076
Nelson, RR	0.451	0.140	0.124	0.081	0.008	0.003	0.306	0.005	0.407	0.452	0.250	0.546	0.184
Nohria, N	0.335	0.101	-0.011	0.037	0.016	-0.028	0.248	-0.038	0.222	0.375	0.229	0.469	0.142
O'Reilly, C	0.531	0.126	0.214	0.323	0.365	0.205	0.474	0.348	0.196	0.389	0.569	0.559	0.343
Palmer, I	0.268	-0.006	-0.011	0.192	-0.015	0.098	0.326	0.015	0.069	0.336	0.304	0.081	0.158
Pasmore, WA	0.431	-0.029	0.391	0.430	0.306	0.278	0.517	0.438	-0.025	0.144	0.357	0.030	0.350
Pettigrew, AM	0.712	0.057	0.197	0.479	0.077	0.224	0.568	0.176	0.316	0.645	0.635	0.361	0.548
Poole, MS	0.488	-0.031	0.023	0.161	0.058	0.084	0.341	0.083	0.299	0.490	0.438	0.214	0.154
Porras, JI	0.413	-0.025	0.491	0.583	0.180	0.313	0.403	0.515	-0.053	0.146	0.386	-0.035	0.458
Potter, J	0.242	-0.049	0.075	0.212	-0.008	0.125	0.269	0.198	0.021	0.253	0.284	0.032	0.150
Powell, WW	0.311	0.034	-0.005	0.043	0.024	-0.023	0.211	-0.049	0.303	0.385	0.174	0.503	0.126
Prasad, P	0.384	-0.040	0.136	0.316	0.016	0.130	0.416	0.099	0.200	0.406	0.371	0.195	0.335
Prochaska, JO	-0.087	-0.037	0.008	-0.020	-0.028	-0.005	-0.049	0.084	-0.055	-0.078	-0.052	-0.074	-0.084
Quinn, RW	0.187	0.208	-0.049	0.026	0.150	0.000	0.170	0.047	0.163	0.268	0.227	0.251	0.010
Rajagopalan, N	0.408	0.165	-0.075	-0.009	0.055	-0.070	0.153	-0.085	0.390	0.494	0.250	0.661	0.137
Reger, R	0.351	-0.001	-0.024	0.066	0.020	-0.016	0.233	-0.047	0.202	0.932	0.309	0.336	0.126
Romanelli, E	0.669	0.016	0.000	0.087	0.008	0.024	0.248	-0.020	0.266	0.440	0.484	0.399	0.174
Rousseau, D	0.370	0.035	0.225	0.338	0.405	0.195	0.437	0.345	0.152	0.248	0.470	0.302	0.297
Sashkin, M	0.382	0.060	0.379	0.543	0.250	0.592	0.425	0.589	-0.053	0.081	0.313	0.026	0.418
Schaffer, RH	0.439	0.090	0.320	0.451	0.281	0.265	0.454	0.384	0.019	0.218	0.356	0.150	0.459
Schein, E	0.628	0.107	0.515	0.716	0.224	0.466	0.742	0.524	0.095	0.394	0.601	0.234	0.628
Sebastian, JG	0.006	-0.033	-0.049	-0.038	-0.032	-0.039	-0.026	-0.084	-0.019	0.077	0.061	0.063	-0.050
Senge, PM	0.462	0.045	0.361	0.483	0.085	0.308	0.651	0.314	0.104	0.395	0.349	0.158	0.462

Appendix C (Cont.)

Co-citation Correlation Matrix

	Greiner, L	Greve, MS	Harris, RT	Harrison, Roger	Heneman, RL	Hersey, P	Hirschhorn, L	Hornstein, H	Hough, JR	Huff, AS	Huy, QN	Jensen, MC	Kakabadse, A
Shani, R	0.214	0.008	0.130	0.189	0.190	0.129	0.265	0.113	0.064	0.287	0.117	0.105	0.186
Shortell, SM	0.351	0.018	-0.023	0.060	0.088	-0.024	0.229	0.000	0.236	0.387	0.213	0.516	0.127
Sproull, LS	0.149	-0.030	0.016	0.068	0.021	0.019	0.142	0.015	0.099	0.234	0.122	0.067	0.046
Stacey, RD	0.521	0.006	0.183	0.338	0.014	0.169	0.550	0.117	0.223	0.492	0.382	0.204	0.321
Stevenson, WB	0.520	0.128	0.125	0.217	0.346	0.131	0.391	0.159	0.338	0.383	0.409	0.526	0.312
Stewart, WH	0.429	0.136	0.114	0.198	0.043	0.107	0.301	0.217	0.314	0.355	0.288	0.383	0.156
Stimpert, JL	0.255	0.021	-0.010	0.023	-0.024	-0.034	0.157	0.008	0.134	0.822	0.229	0.301	0.055
Tannenbaum, R	0.342	0.019	0.395	0.476	0.130	0.820	0.374	0.562	-0.096	0.050	0.202	-0.043	0.377
Tsoukas, H	0.443	-0.012	0.055	0.253	0.005	0.086	0.438	0.024	0.244	0.543	0.420	0.225	0.201
Tushman, M	0.738	0.041	0.107	0.187	0.062	0.078	0.433	0.056	0.455	0.601	0.508	0.532	0.284
Van de Ven, AH	0.709	0.011	0.091	0.203	0.096	0.077	0.467	0.080	0.421	0.599	0.493	0.473	0.287
van Dick, R	0.058	-0.044	0.077	0.134	0.111	0.112	0.126	0.248	0.042	0.053	0.241	0.023	0.076
Walton, RE	0.525	0.023	0.403	0.494	0.403	0.421	0.615	0.534	0.050	0.194	0.331	0.210	0.447
Weick, KE	0.686	0.018	0.222	0.385	0.124	0.201	0.617	0.213	0.436	0.695	0.548	0.423	0.395
White, MC	0.486	0.022	0.120	0.189	0.114	0.195	0.331	0.207	0.153	0.308	0.402	0.398	0.312
Winter, SG	0.228	0.138	0.129	0.010	-0.016	-0.037	0.170	-0.049	0.334	0.269	0.089	0.420	0.104
Woodman, R	0.543	-0.035	0.329	0.495	0.287	0.270	0.496	0.443	0.141	0.360	0.566	0.189	0.458
Wruck, KH	0.050	0.548	-0.054	-0.055	0.056	-0.047	-0.029	-0.033	-0.017	0.030	-0.050	0.717	-0.006
Zajac, EJ	0.411	0.197	-0.067	-0.015	0.046	-0.066	0.171	-0.077	0.252	0.505	0.191	0.803	0.103

Appendix C (Cont.)

Co-citation Correlation Matrix

	Kanter, RM	Kiesler, S	Kim, WC	Kotter, J	Langley, A	Lawler, EE	Lawrence, PR	Ledford, GE	Lewin, K	Lorsch, JW	Mathews, J	Mauborgne, R	Miller, RH
Hirschhorn, L													
Hornstein, H													
Hough, JR													
Huff, AS													
Huy, QN													
Jensen, MC													
Kakabadse, A													
Kanter, RM	1.000												
Kiesler, S	0.403	1.000											
Kim, WC	0.235	0.116	1.000										
Kotter, J	0.833	0.278	0.120	1.000									
Langley, A	0.439	0.333	0.158	0.323	1.000								
Lawler, EE	0.781	0.270	0.089	0.636	0.144	1.000							
Lawrence, PR	0.719	0.450	0.254	0.537	0.494	0.505	1.000						
Ledford, GE	0.486	0.133	0.017	0.382	0.087	0.794	0.278	1.000					
Lewin, K	0.542	0.255	0.004	0.524	0.129	0.629	0.302	0.366	1.000				
Lorsch, JW	0.396	0.174	0.173	0.323	0.201	0.345	0.519	0.148	0.116	1.000			
Mathews, J	0.447	0.175	0.164	0.292	0.146	0.530	0.442	0.480	0.329	0.272	1.000		
Mauborgne, R	0.132	0.060	0.908	0.080	0.050	0.071	0.106	0.020	0.015	0.056	0.020	1.000	
Miller, RH	0.021	0.007	-0.029	-0.011	0.030	0.011	0.049	-0.015	0.059	0.015	0.039	-0.039	1.000
Mirvis, P	0.653	0.173	0.069	0.537	0.103	0.798	0.342	0.603	0.473	0.188	0.358	0.067	-0.026
Moore, L	0.034	0.027	-0.071	0.005	-0.062	0.078	-0.055	0.030	0.283	-0.060	0.075	-0.049	0.176
Morrison, EW	0.506	0.228	0.121	0.444	0.118	0.570	0.230	0.357	0.400	0.150	0.174	0.113	0.172

Appendix C (Cont.)

Co-citation Correlation Matrix

	Kanter, RM	Kiesler, S	Kim, WC	Kotter, J	Langley, A	Lawler, EE	Lawrence, PR	Ledford, GE	Lewin, K	Lorsch, JW	Mathews, J	Mauborgne, R	Miller, RH
Mouton, JS	0.185	0.053	0.011	0.127	0.001	0.173	0.154	0.053	0.210	0.056	0.024	-0.002	-0.027
Nelson, RR	0.435	0.354	0.336	0.252	0.404	0.212	0.571	0.087	0.157	0.291	0.405	0.120	0.006
Nohria, N	0.444	0.273	0.571	0.258	0.365	0.182	0.507	0.084	0.065	0.246	0.410	0.283	0.000
O'Reilly, C	0.862	0.477	0.267	0.638	0.357	0.745	0.599	0.468	0.431	0.523	0.354	0.169	0.040
Palmer, I	0.332	0.164	0.045	0.309	0.405	0.132	0.259	0.071	0.167	0.072	0.128	0.012	-0.011
Pasmore, WA	0.569	0.195	-0.041	0.542	0.145	0.707	0.400	0.629	0.491	0.111	0.378	-0.020	-0.047
Pettigrew, AM	0.770	0.411	0.201	0.693	0.770	0.440	0.704	0.249	0.385	0.382	0.283	0.091	-0.006
Poole, MS	0.493	0.735	0.138	0.344	0.541	0.274	0.527	0.164	0.243	0.175	0.215	0.053	0.002
Porras, JI	0.461	0.116	-0.061	0.505	0.109	0.548	0.272	0.383	0.538	0.069	0.205	-0.020	-0.057
Potter, J	0.304	0.231	0.015	0.251	0.312	0.195	0.183	0.093	0.423	0.010	0.158	-0.005	0.036
Powell, WW	0.399	0.235	0.257	0.184	0.428	0.153	0.450	0.078	0.068	0.225	0.372	0.049	0.044
Prasad, P	0.502	0.415	0.085	0.389	0.458	0.275	0.422	0.140	0.293	0.138	0.169	0.015	0.000
Prochaska, JO	-0.053	-0.010	-0.064	-0.058	-0.079	-0.007	-0.082	-0.020	0.174	-0.070	0.084	-0.042	0.169
Quinn, RW	0.241	0.328	0.112	0.228	0.235	0.213	0.268	0.163	0.136	0.207	0.190	0.059	0.177
Rajagopalan, N	0.350	0.290	0.344	0.211	0.434	0.185	0.450	0.080	0.045	0.560	0.192	0.178	0.089
Reger, R	0.332	0.355	0.187	0.245	0.417	0.152	0.408	0.069	0.128	0.236	0.147	0.053	0.031
Romanelli, E	0.452	0.318	0.203	0.323	0.504	0.177	0.537	0.106	0.119	0.326	0.169	0.067	-0.003
Rousseau, D	0.696	0.304	0.173	0.554	0.239	0.725	0.430	0.489	0.408	0.257	0.261	0.130	0.235
Sashkin, M	0.581	0.099	-0.031	0.654	0.080	0.614	0.279	0.430	0.493	0.132	0.231	-0.011	-0.052
Schaffer, RH	0.547	0.161	0.069	0.615	0.161	0.556	0.366	0.390	0.449	0.168	0.477	0.047	0.008
Schein, E	0.876	0.344	0.121	0.867	0.336	0.743	0.579	0.434	0.675	0.313	0.335	0.085	0.018
Sebastian, JG	0.001	-0.002	0.007	-0.020	0.195	-0.051	0.010	-0.033	-0.030	-0.010	-0.004	-0.028	0.047
Senge, PM	0.583	0.302	0.124	0.580	0.251	0.478	0.451	0.271	0.444	0.181	0.364	0.080	0.025

Co-citation Correlation Matrix

	Kanter, RM	Kiesler, S	Kim, WC	Kotter, J	Langley, A	Lawler, EE	Lawrence, PR	Ledford, GE	Lewin, K	Lorsch, JW	Mathews, J	Mauborgne, R	Miller, RH
Shani, R	0.285	0.116	0.000	0.294	0.118	0.339	0.299	0.382	0.176	0.075	0.363	-0.034	-0.021
Shortell, SM	0.418	0.250	0.199	0.260	0.378	0.282	0.471	0.156	0.095	0.373	0.209	0.053	0.570
Sproull, LS	0.193	0.822	0.024	0.140	0.139	0.106	0.211	0.037	0.106	0.066	0.014	0.013	0.003
Stacey, RD	0.526	0.323	0.143	0.466	0.494	0.319	0.539	0.160	0.327	0.190	0.295	0.070	0.022
Stevenson, WB	0.677	0.396	0.291	0.517	0.417	0.556	0.658	0.398	0.257	0.480	0.384	0.136	-0.008
Stewart, WH	0.488	0.432	0.216	0.353	0.402	0.340	0.539	0.150	0.329	0.338	0.371	0.096	0.099
Stimpert, JL	0.227	0.311	0.169	0.140	0.312	0.102	0.283	0.017	0.165	0.240	0.113	0.055	0.014
Tannenbaum, R	0.386	0.063	-0.027	0.466	-0.001	0.445	0.246	0.262	0.553	0.090	0.127	0.012	-0.062
Tsoukas, H	0.463	0.385	0.191	0.361	0.604	0.226	0.498	0.120	0.237	0.155	0.206	0.096	-0.027
Tushman, M	0.691	0.517	0.319	0.483	0.625	0.378	0.831	0.204	0.227	0.427	0.388	0.130	0.015
Van de Ven, AH	0.719	0.516	0.341	0.475	0.656	0.410	0.847	0.244	0.248	0.376	0.443	0.143	0.037
van Dick, R	0.244	0.171	0.040	0.206	0.006	0.332	0.084	0.146	0.367	0.009	-0.017	0.083	0.229
Walton, RE	0.700	0.256	0.074	0.582	0.181	0.843	0.576	0.705	0.503	0.272	0.456	0.050	-0.025
Weick, KE	0.795	0.660	0.246	0.625	0.643	0.534	0.836	0.307	0.428	0.378	0.419	0.110	0.035
White, MC	0.627	0.338	0.144	0.459	0.289	0.397	0.454	0.182	0.253	0.396	0.174	0.083	-0.018
Winter, SG	0.224	0.189	0.277	0.105	0.208	0.085	0.339	0.009	0.047	0.143	0.313	0.095	-0.013
Woodman, R	0.765	0.320	0.105	0.621	0.460	0.678	0.496	0.454	0.526	0.201	0.323	0.073	-0.010
Wruck, KH	0.039	0.021	0.090	0.030	-0.007	0.102	0.066	-0.002	-0.042	0.608	0.220	0.006	0.021
Zajac, EJ	0.412	0.286	0.332	0.216	0.432	0.210	0.504	0.090	0.033	0.634	0.299	0.106	0.260

Appendix C (Cont.)

Co-citation Correlation Matrix

	Mirvis, P	Moore, L	Morrison, EW	Mouton, JS	Nelson, RR	Nohria, N	O'Reilly, C	Palmer, I	Pasmore, WA	Pettigrew, AM	Poole, MS	Porras, JI	Potter, J
Hirschhorn, L													
Hornstein, H													
Hough, JR													
Huff, AS													
Huy, QN													
Jensen, MC													
Kakabadse, A													
Kanter, RM													
Kiesler, S													
Kim, WC													
Kotter, J													
Langley, A													
Lawler, EE													
Lawrence, PR													
Ledford, GE													
Lewin, K													
Lorsch, JW													
Mathews, J													
Mauborgne, R													
Miller, RH													
Mirvis, P	1.000												
Moore, L	0.018	1.000											
Morrison, EW	0.483	0.109	1.000										

Co-citation Correlation Matrix

	Mirvis, P	Moore, L	Morrison, EW	Mouton, JS	Nelson, RR	Nohria, N	O'Reilly, C	Palmer, I	Pasmore, WA	Pettigrew, AM	Poole, MS	Porras, JI	Potter, J
Mouton, JS	0.286	-0.020	0.078	1.000									
Nelson, RR	0.123	-0.047	0.131	0.021	1.000								
Nohria, N	0.142	-0.069	0.156	0.040	0.532	1.000							
O'Reilly, C	0.594	0.069	0.647	0.137	0.403	0.401	1.000						
Palmer, I	0.132	-0.039	0.119	0.021	0.161	0.186	0.195	1.000					
Pasmore, WA	0.698	-0.030	0.280	0.112	0.114	0.065	0.405	0.180	1.000				
Pettigrew, AM	0.361	-0.044	0.299	0.085	0.491	0.431	0.609	0.488	0.391	1.000			
Poole, MS	0.190	-0.029	0.204	0.052	0.389	0.346	0.454	0.321	0.308	0.587	1.000		
Porras, JI	0.601	0.012	0.232	0.126	0.067	0.016	0.299	0.084	0.678	0.338	0.180	1.000	
Potter, J	0.169	0.186	0.190	0.049	0.121	0.123	0.210	0.650	0.177	0.382	0.270	0.119	1.000
Powell, WW	0.119	-0.033	0.118	0.045	0.536	0.599	0.335	0.230	0.043	0.426	0.301	0.021	0.209
Prasad, P	0.249	-0.004	0.244	0.040	0.310	0.325	0.384	0.491	0.274	0.621	0.567	0.194	0.467
Prochaska, JO	-0.042	0.708	0.030	-0.028	-0.048	-0.073	-0.024	-0.067	-0.064	-0.092	-0.051	-0.007	0.120
Quinn, RW	0.173	0.001	0.191	0.027	0.301	0.162	0.310	0.152	0.149	0.283	0.320	0.089	0.172
Rajagopalan, N	0.070	-0.076	0.131	-0.032	0.428	0.432	0.496	0.133	0.006	0.460	0.322	-0.027	0.057
Reger, R	0.093	-0.044	0.130	-0.018	0.386	0.370	0.355	0.235	0.062	0.482	0.379	0.071	0.156
Romanelli, E	0.091	-0.065	0.127	-0.014	0.585	0.373	0.485	0.141	0.137	0.553	0.392	0.092	0.082
Rousseau, D	0.630	0.081	0.856	0.125	0.223	0.275	0.802	0.186	0.414	0.448	0.334	0.296	0.203
Sashkin, M	0.529	-0.001	0.302	0.178	0.056	0.037	0.403	0.098	0.531	0.349	0.121	0.549	0.134
Schaffer, RH	0.451	-0.020	0.284	0.035	0.240	0.182	0.395	0.138	0.427	0.434	0.187	0.486	0.132
Schein, E	0.658	0.037	0.596	0.196	0.307	0.269	0.705	0.350	0.591	0.734	0.398	0.583	0.332
Sebastian, JG	-0.034	-0.033	-0.022	0.035	0.053	0.071	-0.007	0.044	-0.070	0.112	0.046	-0.048	0.216
Senge, PM	0.387	-0.006	0.296	0.106	0.366	0.270	0.359	0.290	0.434	0.518	0.341	0.435	0.195

Appendix C (Cont.)

Co-citation Correlation Matrix

	Mirvis, P	Moore, L	Morrison, EW	Mouton, JS	Nelson, RR	Nohria, N	O'Reilly, C	Palmer, I	Pasmore, WA	Pettigrew, AM	Poole, MS	Porras, JI	Potter, J
Shani, R	0.232	-0.075	0.078	-0.021	0.185	0.143	0.171	0.078	0.239	0.251	0.136	0.195	0.022
Shortell, SM	0.207	0.030	0.362	0.010	0.362	0.409	0.503	0.177	0.101	0.402	0.292	0.015	0.130
Sproull, LS	0.077	-0.029	0.107	0.028	0.164	0.101	0.237	0.095	0.080	0.222	0.426	0.021	0.148
Stacey, RD	0.275	-0.062	0.198	0.046	0.452	0.332	0.344	0.373	0.334	0.637	0.461	0.288	0.275
Stevenson, WB	0.414	-0.042	0.327	0.081	0.466	0.519	0.708	0.228	0.343	0.611	0.417	0.183	0.183
Stewart, WH	0.187	0.082	0.260	0.072	0.424	0.348	0.508	0.174	0.172	0.463	0.457	0.136	0.211
Stimpert, JL	0.029	0.010	0.088	-0.018	0.325	0.263	0.269	0.142	-0.003	0.352	0.301	0.035	0.138
Tannenbaum, R	0.397	-0.011	0.185	0.414	0.009	-0.025	0.203	0.074	0.398	0.239	0.066	0.461	0.140
Tsoukas, H	0.204	-0.055	0.182	0.044	0.480	0.404	0.345	0.646	0.259	0.656	0.547	0.176	0.476
Tushman, M	0.238	-0.064	0.235	0.046	0.783	0.575	0.653	0.252	0.271	0.751	0.607	0.179	0.171
Van de Ven, AH	0.282	-0.050	0.263	0.069	0.680	0.658	0.627	0.338	0.336	0.764	0.756	0.193	0.234
van Dick, R	0.319	0.184	0.520	0.133	-0.007	-0.011	0.366	0.016	0.134	0.081	0.091	0.141	0.156
Walton, RE	0.707	-0.015	0.337	0.307	0.217	0.182	0.556	0.147	0.749	0.460	0.323	0.572	0.127
Weick, KE	0.414	-0.004	0.382	0.107	0.628	0.516	0.697	0.443	0.426	0.842	0.707	0.332	0.381
White, MC	0.283	0.061	0.264	0.068	0.288	0.230	0.654	0.122	0.184	0.476	0.298	0.148	0.139
Winter, SG	0.041	-0.062	0.054	-0.004	0.918	0.371	0.195	0.066	0.020	0.265	0.200	-0.008	0.023
Woodman, R	0.624	0.029	0.401	0.151	0.289	0.243	0.648	0.263	0.640	0.656	0.485	0.685	0.234
Wruck, KH	0.017	-0.046	0.022	-0.004	0.157	0.055	0.217	-0.022	-0.078	0.040	0.002	-0.086	-0.055
Zajac, EJ	0.105	-0.053	0.149	0.005	0.541	0.561	0.539	0.162	0.013	0.463	0.330	-0.047	0.088

109

Co-citation Correlation Matrix

	Powell, WW	Prasad, P	Prochaska, JO	Quinn, RW	Rajagopalan, N	Reger, R	Romanelli, E	Rousseau, D	Sashkin, M	Schaffer, RH	Schein, E	Sebastian, JG	Senge, PM
Mouton, JS													
Nelson, RR													
Nohria, N													
OReilly, C													
Palmer, I													
Pasmore, WA													
Pettigrew, AM													
Poole, MS													
Porras, JI													
Potter, J													
Powell, WW	1.000												
Prasad, P	0.480	1.000											
Prochaska, JO	-0.051	-0.066	1.000										
Quinn, RW	0.111	0.125	-0.009	1.000									
Rajagopalan, N	0.366	0.198	-0.083	0.224	1.000								
Reger, R	0.396	0.306	-0.069	0.178	0.495	1.000							
Romanelli, E	0.409	0.264	-0.063	0.201	0.514	0.401	1.000						
Rousseau, D	0.208	0.325	-0.023	0.265	0.264	0.225	0.245	1.000					
Sashkin, M	0.032	0.180	-0.043	0.054	-0.030	0.045	0.107	0.405	1.000				
Schaffer, RH	0.145	0.227	-0.060	0.133	0.104	0.182	0.213	0.351	0.459	1.000			
Schein, E	0.230	0.534	-0.049	0.202	0.209	0.272	0.294	0.685	0.620	0.609	1.000		
Sebastian, JG	0.165	0.055	-0.030	0.089	0.043	0.050	0.046	-0.006	-0.052	-0.043	-0.006	1.000	
Senge, PM	0.184	0.388	-0.034	0.250	0.171	0.255	0.223	0.345	0.392	0.535	0.726	-0.019	1.000

Appendix C (Cont.)

Co-citation Correlation Matrix

	Powell, WW	Prasad, P	Prochaska, JO	Quinn, RW	Rajagopalan, N	Reger, R	Romanelli, E	Rousseau, D	Sashkin, M	Schaffer, RH	Schein, E	Sebastian, JG	Senge, PM
Shani, R	0.202	0.172	-0.080	0.067	0.060	0.351	0.097	0.157	0.216	0.609	0.307	-0.033	0.285
Shortell, SM	0.482	0.295	-0.037	0.230	0.595	0.430	0.371	0.591	0.065	0.149	0.303	0.114	0.200
Sproull, LS	0.105	0.213	-0.031	0.213	0.101	0.179	0.132	0.148	0.032	0.060	0.186	0.004	0.143
Stacey, RD	0.306	0.435	-0.076	0.257	0.301	0.328	0.401	0.295	0.235	0.392	0.568	0.033	0.692
Stevenson, WB	0.365	0.341	-0.085	0.301	0.530	0.335	0.452	0.496	0.282	0.331	0.503	0.043	0.286
Stewart, WH	0.256	0.262	0.036	0.332	0.440	0.275	0.373	0.363	0.155	0.215	0.393	-0.042	0.335
Stimpert, JL	0.261	0.174	-0.010	0.179	0.454	0.755	0.322	0.131	-0.017	0.074	0.176	0.042	0.222
Tannenbaum, R	-0.016	0.141	-0.042	-0.019	-0.072	-0.007	0.017	0.220	0.548	0.347	0.519	-0.063	0.325
Tsoukas, H	0.360	0.597	-0.069	0.317	0.288	0.390	0.343	0.273	0.114	0.236	0.465	0.049	0.473
Tushman, M	0.537	0.426	-0.084	0.316	0.580	0.511	0.835	0.411	0.190	0.326	0.500	0.067	0.415
Van de Ven, AH	0.567	0.509	-0.077	0.324	0.539	0.506	0.661	0.467	0.188	0.299	0.513	0.059	0.427
van Dick, R	-0.012	0.070	0.135	0.142	0.031	0.055	-0.002	0.606	0.160	0.108	0.294	-0.039	0.106
Walton, RE	0.150	0.282	-0.063	0.157	0.125	0.132	0.192	0.510	0.556	0.486	0.665	-0.058	0.434
Weick, KE	0.526	0.642	-0.067	0.375	0.478	0.553	0.543	0.546	0.316	0.423	0.729	0.059	0.618
White, MC	0.233	0.221	0.010	0.125	0.491	0.275	0.477	0.373	0.242	0.205	0.420	-0.014	0.223
Winter, SG	0.332	0.141	-0.050	0.209	0.246	0.217	0.344	0.100	-0.016	0.150	0.156	0.033	0.252
Woodman, R	0.197	0.373	-0.031	0.281	0.223	0.252	0.320	0.561	0.521	0.466	0.688	-0.010	0.457
Wruck, KH	0.061	-0.049	-0.033	0.250	0.352	0.053	0.114	0.039	-0.048	0.002	-0.005	-0.027	-0.011
Zajac, EJ	0.602	0.279	-0.077	0.228	0.822	0.547	0.536	0.333	-0.012	0.123	0.217	0.113	0.171

Appendix C (Cont.)

Co-citation Correlation Matrix

	Shani, R	Shortell, SM	Sproull, LS	Stacey, RD	Stevenson, WB	Stewart, WH	Stimpert, JL	Tannenbaum, R	Tsoukas, H	Tushman, M	Van de Ven, AH	van Dick, R	Walton, RE
Shani, R	1.000												
Shortell, SM	0.127	1.000											
Sproull, LS	0.035	0.085	1.000										
Stacey, RD	0.207	0.290	0.136	1.000									
Stevenson, WB	0.222	0.453	0.173	0.357	1.000								
Stewart, WH	0.101	0.358	0.151	0.396	0.435	1.000							
Stimpert, JL	0.105	0.299	0.142	0.279	0.215	0.278	1.000						
Tannenbaum, R	0.167	-0.029	0.024	0.184	0.139	0.081	-0.038	1.000					
Tsoukas, H	0.171	0.271	0.197	0.654	0.412	0.401	0.278	0.085	1.000				
Tushman, M	0.219	0.497	0.239	0.566	0.652	0.566	0.395	0.081	0.542	1.000			
Van de Ven, AH	0.231	0.538	0.210	0.580	0.653	0.575	0.388	0.086	0.598	0.911	1.000		
van Dick, R	-0.015	0.362	0.092	0.069	0.103	0.133	0.022	0.116	0.046	0.062	0.084	1.000	
Walton, RE	0.358	0.205	0.119	0.321	0.514	0.271	0.055	0.513	0.241	0.386	0.438	0.147	1.000
Weick, KE	0.311	0.504	0.335	0.681	0.665	0.614	0.420	0.226	0.716	0.844	0.868	0.176	0.520
White, MC	0.046	0.347	0.163	0.269	0.481	0.359	0.248	0.127	0.204	0.530	0.470	0.119	0.300
Winter, SG	0.121	0.193	0.080	0.293	0.284	0.275	0.184	-0.037	0.339	0.550	0.421	-0.040	0.096
Woodman, R	0.195	0.263	0.122	0.420	0.468	0.373	0.194	0.336	0.401	0.508	0.570	0.220	0.603
Wruck, KH	-0.014	0.119	-0.013	-0.005	0.175	0.178	0.105	-0.072	-0.003	0.091	0.055	-0.038	0.012
Zajac, EJ	0.118	0.802	0.103	0.294	0.559	0.441	0.454	-0.080	0.315	0.635	0.611	0.070	0.148

Co-citation Correlation Matrix

	Weick, KE	White, MC	Winter, SG	Woodman, R	Wruck, KH	Zajac, EJ
Shani, R						
Shortell, SM						
Sproull, LS						
Stacey, RD						
Stevenson, WB						
Stewart, WH						
Stimpert, JL						
Tannenbaum, R						
Tsoukas, H						
Tushman, M						
Van de Ven, AH						
van Dick, R						
Walton, RE						
Weick, KE	1.000					
White, MC	0.478	1.000				
Winter, SG	0.387	0.108	1.000			
Woodman, R	0.617	0.442	0.139	1.000		
Wruck, KH	0.032	0.138	0.099	-0.042	1.000	
Zajac, EJ	0.526	0.451	0.339	0.220	0.390	1.000

Retained Factors from First Analysis

	Initial Eigenvalues		
Factor	Total	% of Variance	Cumulative %
1	40.306	36.312	36.312
2	36.822	33.173	69.485
3	6.161	5.551	75.035
4	5.306	4.780	79.816
5	2.695	2.428	82.243
6	2.491	2.244	84.487
7	2.240	2.018	86.505
8	2.018	1.818	88.323
9	1.596	1.438	89.761
10	1.528	1.376	91.137
11	1.303	1.174	92.311
12	1.026	0.924	93.235
	Extraction Sums of Squared Loadings		
Factor	Total	% of Variance	Cumulative %
1	40.306	36.312	36.312
2	36.822	33.173	69.485
3	6.161	5.551	75.035
4	5.306	4.780	79.816
5	2.695	2.428	82.243
6	2.491	2.244	84.487
7	2.240	2.018	86.505
8	2.018	1.818	88.323
9	1.596	1.438	89.761
10	1.528	1.376	91.137
11	1.303	1.174	92.311
12	1.026	0.924	93.235
	Rotation Sums of Squared Loadings		
Factor	Total	% of Variance	Cumulative %
1	38.072	34.299	34.299
2	34.038	30.665	64.964
3	5.622	5.065	70.029
4	5.044	4.544	74.573
5	4.435	3.996	78.569
6	3.545	3.194	81.763
7	3.402	3.065	84.828
8	2.464	2.220	87.048
9	1.861	1.677	88.725
10	1.792	1.615	90.339
11	1.713	1.543	91.882
12	1.502	1.353	93.235

Appendix E

Total Variance Explained by Reduced Co-citation Factors

Factor	Extraction Sums of Squared Loadings			Rotation Sums of Squared Loadings		
	Total	% of Variance	Cumulative %	Total	% of Variance	Cumulative %
1	40.306	36.312	36.312	37.818	34.070	34.070
2	36.822	33.173	69.485	34.930	31.469	65.539
3	6.161	5.551	75.035	6.167	5.556	71.095
4	5.306	4.780	79.816	5.562	5.011	76.106
5	2.695	2.428	82.243	5.081	4.577	80.683
6	2.491	2.244	84.487	4.223	3.804	84.487

Rotated Component Matrix for Co-citation Data

	Component					
	1	2	3	4	5	6
Bennis, Warren	.976					
Beer, Michael	.956					
Beckhard, Richard	.953					
Harrison, Roger	.951					
French, Wendell	.951					
Coch, Lester	.932					
Burke, Warner W.	.931					
Sashkin, Marshall	.930					
Porras, Jerry I.	.918					
Walton, Richard E.	.917					
Goodstein, Leonard D.	.915					
Golembiewski, Robert T.	.915					
Blake, Robert R.	.915					
Pasmore, William A.	.909					
Benne, Kenneth D.	.909					
Dunphy, Dexter	.908					
Kakabadse, Andrew	.907					
Schein, Edgar	.906					
Cummings, Thomas G.	.903					
Tannenbaum, Robert	.899					
Harris, Reuben T.	.897					
Bushe, Gervase	.888					
Lewin, Kurt	.881					
Schaffer, Robert H.	.881					
Kotter, John	.877					
Argyris, Chris	.869	.436				
Hornstein, Harvey	.866					
Mirvis, Phil	.866		.430			
Conger, Jay A.	.846					
Lawler, Edward E. III	.844		.481			
Hirschhorn, Larry	.840	.437				
Eddy, William	.836					
Hersey, Paul	.829					
Cooperrider, David	.824					
Woodman, Richard	.798					
Cohen, Allan R.	.792		.433			
Senge, Peter M.	.772	.456				
Ledford, Gerald E. Jr.	.729		.499			
Kanter, Rosabeth Moss	.709	.594				
Brown, L. Dave	.693					
Beer, Stafford	.670	.569				
Shani, Rami	.560					

Rotated Component Matrix for Co-citation Data

	Component					
	1	2	3	4	5	6
Mouton, Jane S.	.515					
Sebastian, JG						
Daft, Richard L.		.955				
Van de Ven, Andrew H.		.953				
Weick, Karl E.		.950				
Ford, Jeffrey D.		.948				
Tushman, Michael		.939				
Langley, Ann		.934				
Gray, Barbara		.912				
Poole, Marshall Scott		.910				
Huff, Anne S.		.902				
Bower, Josph L.		.901				
Greenwood, Royston		.901				
Pettigrew, Andrew M.		.894				
Tsoukas, Hari		.884				
Romanelli, Elaine		.879				
Galbraith, Jay R.		.876				
Lawrence, Paul R.		.875				
Stewart, Wayne H.		.852				
Reger, Rhonda		.845				
Stacey, Ralph D.		.823				
Nelson, Richard R.		.820				
Kiesler, Sara		.811				
Prasad, P.		.807				
Stevenson, William B.		.799				
Barr, Pamela S.		.792				
Bartunek, Jean	.483	.791				
Powell, Walter, W.		.769				
Rajagopalan, Nandini		.766		.405		
Hough, Jill R.		.766				
Boeker, Warren		.756		.455		
DiMaggio, Paul		.747				
Zajac, Edward J.	-.419	.744		.432		
Greiner, Larry	.576	.743				
Shortell, Stephen M.		.737				
Stimpert, J. L.		.733				
French, John L.		.715	.407			
Nohria, Nitin		.714				.581
Alvesson, Mats	.444	.705		-.404		
White, Margaret C.		.705				
Palmer, Ian		.689		-.462		
Huy, Quy Nguyen	.498	.657				
O'Reilly, Charles		.650	.569			

Rotated Component Matrix for Co-citation Data

	Component					
	1	2	3	4	5	6
Quinn, Robert W.		.649				
Winter, Sidney G.		.643				
Sproull, Lee S.		.566				
Bedeian, Arthur	.541		.757			
Rousseau, Denise M.	.491		.706			
Morrison, Elizabeth Wolfe	.489		.700			
Heneman, Robert L.	.455		.680			
van Dick, Rolf			.636		-.410	
Armenakis, Achilles A.	.488		.580			
Wruck, Karen Hopper				.763		
Lorsch, Jay W.		.569		.718		
Greve, Michael S.				.674		
Jensen, Michael C.		.609		.624		
Potter, J.		.460		-.613		
Mathews, J.				.410		
Bandura, Albert					-.850	
Davis, David A.					-.838	
Moore, Linda					-.838	
Prochaska, J. O.					-.795	
DiClemente, C. C.					-.790	
Miller, RH					-.546	
Bartlett, Christopher A.		.532				.736
Kim, W. Chan						.732
Mauborgne, Renee						.712
Ghoshal, Sumantra		.653				.656
Adler, Nancy J.	.402	.508				.600

Bibliography

Alderfer, C. P. (1977). Organization development. *Annual Review of Psychology, 28,*

197-223.

Anderson, C. W., & Campbell, T. L. (2004). Corporate governance of Japanese banks.

Journal of Corporate Finance, 10(3), 327-354.

Angle, H. L., Manz, C. C., & Vandeven, A. H. (1985). Integrating human-resource

management and corporate-strategy - a preview of the 3M story. *Human resource*

management, 24(1), 51-68.

Armenakis, A. A., & Bedeian, A. G. (1999). Organizational change: A review of theory

and research in the 1990s. *Journal of Management, 25*(3), 293-315.

Armenakis, A. A., Harris, S. G., & Feild, H. S. (1999). Making change permanent:

Institutionalizing change interventions. In R. W. Woodman, & W. A. Pasmore

(Eds.), *Research in organizational change and development* (Vol. 12 ed., pp. 97-

128). Stamford, CT: JAI Press, Inc.

Armenakis, A. A., & Harris, S. G. (2002). Crafting a change message to create

transformational readiness. *Journal of Organizational Change Management, 15*(2),

169-183.

Armenakis, A. A., Harris, S. G., & Mossholder, K. W. (1993). Creating readiness for

organizational change. *Human Relations, 46*(6), 681-703.

Astley, W. G., & Vandeven, A. H. (1983). Central perspectives and debates in organization theory. *Administrative Science Quarterly, 28*(2), 245-273.

Bandura, A. (2004). Health promotion by social cognitive means. *Health Education & Behavior, 31*(2), 143-164.

Barnett, W. P., & Carroll, G. R. (1995). Modeling internal organizational change. *Annual Review of Sociology, 21*, 217-236.

Barr, P. S., Stimpert, J. L., & Huff, A. S. (1992). Cognitive change, strategic action, and organizational renewal. *Strategic Management Journal, 13*, 15-36.

Bartlett, C. A., & Ghoshal, S. (1994). Changing the role of top management - beyond strategy to purpose. *Harvard Business Review, 72*(6), 79-88.

Bedeian, A. G., & Feild, H. S. (2002). Assessing group change: Under conditions of anonymity and overlapping samples. *Nursing research, 51*(1), 63-65.

Beer, M. (1976). The technology of organization development. In M. Dunnette (Ed.), *Handbook of industrial and organizational psychology* (pp. 937-993). Chicago, IL: Rand McNally.

Beer, M., & Walton, A. E. (1987). Organization change and development. *Annual Review of Psychology, 38*, 339-367.

Beer, M., & Nohria, N. (2000). Cracking the code of change. *Harvard Business Review, 78*(3), 133-141.

Bennis, W. G. (1969). *Organization development: Its nature, origins, and prospects.* Reading, Massachusetts: Addison-Wesley.

Bennis, W., & Jamieson, D. (1981). Organization development at the crossroads. *Training and Development Journal, 35*(4), 18-26.

Boter, H., & Holmquist, C. (1996). Industry characteristics and internationalization processes in small firms. *Journal of Business Venturing, 11*(6), 471-487.

Burke, W. W., & Litwin, G. H. (1992). A causal model of organizational performance and change. *Journal of Management, 18*(3), 532-545.

Burke, W. W. (2002). *Organization change: Theory and practice.* Thousand Oaks, CA: Sage Publications.

Burke, W. W., Richley, E. A., & Deangelis, L. (1985). Changing leadership and planning processes at the Lewis research center, National Aeronautics and Space Administration. *Human resource management, 24*(1), 81-90.

Caldwell, C., & Karri, R. (2005). Organizational governance and ethical systems: A covenantal approach to building trust. *Journal of Business Ethics, 58*(1), 249-259.

Chauvin, S. W., & Ellett, C. D. (1993). *Teacher receptivity to change: An empirical examination of construct validity using the results of large-scale factor analyses.* No. ED361379). LaPlace, LA: Southeastern Louisiana University.

Cheng, C. H., Kumar, A., Motwani, J. G., Reisman, A., & Madan, M. S. (1999). A citation analysis of the technology innovation management journals. *IEEE Transactions on Engineering Management, 46*(1), 4-13.

Clarke, J. S., & Others, A. (1996). *Faculty Receptivity/Resistance to change, personal and organizational efficacy, decision deprivation and effectiveness in research I universities. ASHE annual meeting paper.* No. ED402,846)

Conway, J. M., & Huffcutt, A. I. (2003). A review and evaluation of exploratory factor analysis practices in organizational research. *Organizational Research Methods, 6*(2), 147-168.

Culnan, M. J. (1986). The intellectual development of management information systems, 1972-1982: A co-citation analysis. *Management Science, 32*(2), 156-172.

Day, D. V., & Bedeian, A. G. (1991). Predicting job-performance across organizations - the interaction of work orientation and psychological climate. *Journal of Management, 17*(3), 589-600.

Denis, D. J. (1990). Defensive changes in corporate payout policy - share repurchases and special dividends. *Journal of Finance, 45*(5), 1433-1456.

Feinberg, B. J., Ostroff, C., & Burke, W. W. (2005). The role of within-group agreement in understanding transformational leadership. *Journal of Occupational and Organizational Psychology, 78*, 471-488.

Ford, J. K., MacCallum, R. C., & Tait, M. (1986). The application of exploratory factor analysis in applied psychology: A critical review and analysis. *Personnel Psychology, 39*(2), 291-314.

Friedlander, F., & Brown, L. D. (1974). Organization development. *Annual Review of Psychology, 25*, 313-341.

Hannan, M. T., & Freeman, J. O. (1984). Structural inertia and organizational change. *American Sociological Review, 49*(2), 149-164.

Heneman, R. L. (1988). Performance assessment - methods and applications - by ronald A. berk. *Industrial & labor relations review, 41*(3), 480-481.

Hoffman, D. L., & Holbrook, M. B. (1993). The intellectual structure of consumer research: A bibliometric study of author cocitations in the first 15 years of the journal of consumer research. *The Journal of Consumer Research, 19*(4), 505-517.

Huff, A. S. (2000). Changes in organizational knowledge production. *Academy of Management Review, 25*(2), 288-293.

Jarzabkowski, P. (2003). Strategic practices: An activity theory perspective on continuity and change. *Journal of Management Studies, 40*(1), 23-55.

Jensen, M. C. (1993). The modern industrial-revolution, exit, and the failure of internal control-systems. *Journal of Finance, 48*(3), 831-880.

Jordan, M. H., Feild, H. S., & Armenakis, A. A. (2002). The relationship of group process variables and team performance - A team-level analysis in a field setting. *Small Group Research, 33*(1), 121-150.

Kachigan, S. K. (1991). *Multivariate statistical analysis* (2nd ed.). New York, NY: Radius Press.

Kuhn, T. S. (1962). *The structure of scientific revolutions.* Chicago, IL: University of Chicago Press.

Labianca, G., Gray, B., & Brass, D. J. (2000). A grounded model of organizational schema change during empowerment. *Organization Science, 11*(2), 235-257.

Lewin, K. (1947). Frontiers in group dynamics: Concept, method and reality in social science; social equilibria and social change. *Human Relations, 1*(1), 5-41.

Lorenzi, N. M., & Riley, R. T. (2000). Managing change - an overview. *Journal of the American Medical Informatics Association, 7*(2), 116-124.

Markus, M. L., & Robey, D. (1988). Information technology and organizational-change - causal-structure in theory and research. *Management Science, 34*(5), 583-598.

McDougall, P. P., & Oviatt, B. M. (1996). New venture internationalization, strategic change, and performance: A follow-up study. *Journal of Business Venturing, 11*(1), 23-40.

Meyer, J. P., Allen, N. J., & Topolnytsky, L. (1998). Commitment in a changing world of work. *Canadian Psychology-Psychologie Canadienne, 39*(1-2), 83-93.

Moore, L. (1995). Getting past the rapids - individuals and change. *Serials Librarian, 25*(3-4), 95-109.

Moulding, N., Silagy, C., & Weller, D. (1999). A framework for effective management of change in clinical practice: Dissemination and implementation of clinical practice guidelines. *Quality and Safety in Health Care, 8*(3), 177-183.

Pasmore, W. A., & Fagans, M. R. (1992). Participation, individual development and organizational change: A review and synthesis. *Journal of Management, 18*(2), 375-397.

Pilkington, A., & Liston-Heyes, C. (1999). Is production and operations management a discipline? A citation/co-citation study. *International Journal of Operations & Production Management, 19*(1), 7-20.

Porras, J. I., & Robertson, P. J. (1992). Organization development: Theory, practice, and research. In M. D. Dunnette, & L. M. Hough (Eds.), *Handbook of industrial and organizational psychology* (Vol. 3, 2nd ed. ed., pp. 719-822). Palo Alto, CA: Consulting Psychologists Press.

Porras, J. I., & Silvers, R. C. (1991). Organization development and transformation. *Annual Review of Psychology, 42*, 51-78.

Prochaska, J. O., Diclemente, C. C., & Norcross, J. C. (1992). In search of how people change - applications to addictive behaviors. *American Psychologist, 47*(9), 1102-1114.

Rajagopalan, N., & Spreitzer, G. M. (1997). Toward a theory of strategic change: A multi-lens perspective and integrative framework. *The Academy of Management Review, 22*(1), 48-79.

Robertson, P. J., Roberts, D. R., & Porras, J. I. (1993). Dynamics of planned organizational-change - assessing empirical support for a theoretical-model. *Academy of Management Journal, 36*(3), 619-634.

Robinson, S. L., Kraatz, M. S., & Rousseau, D. M. (1994). Changing obligations and the psychological contract - a longitudinal-study. *Academy of Management Journal, 37*(1), 137-152.

Rousseau, D. M. (1998). Why workers still identify with organizations. *Journal of Organizational Behavior, 19*(3), 217-233.

Sashkin, M., & Burke, W. W. (1987). Organization development in the 1980's. *Journal of Management, 13*(2), 393.

Schein, E. H., Beckhard, R., & Driscoll, J. W. (1980). Teaching organizational-psychology to middle managers - a process approach. *Exchange-Organizational Behavior Teaching Journal, 5*(1), 19-26.

Snow, M. G., Prochaska, J. O., & Rossi, J. S. (1994). Processes of change in alcoholics-anonymous - maintenance factors in long-term sobriety. *Journal of studies on alcohol, 55*(3), 362-371.

Sparrowe, R. T., & Liden, R. C. (1997). Process and structure in leader-member exchange. *Academy of Management Review, 22*(2), 522-552.

Spicer, John. (2005). *Making sense of multivariate data analysis.* Thousand Oaks, CA: Sage Publications.

Tabachnick, B. G., & Fidell, L. S. (1983). *Using multivariate statistics.* New York, NY: Harper & Row.

Thomson Scientific. (2006). *Social sciences citation index.* Retrieved May 11, 2006, from http://scientific.thomson.com/products/ssci/

Van de Ven, A.H., & Poole, M. S. (1995). Explaining development and change in organizations. *The Academy of Management Review, 20*(3), 510-540.

Walton, R. E. (1980). Planned changes to improve organizational-effectiveness. *Technology in Society, 2*(4), 391-412.

Waugh, R., & Godfrey, J. (1995). Understanding teachers' receptivity to system-wide educational change. *Journal of Education Administration, 33*(3), 38-54.

White, H. D., & Griffith, B. C. (1981). Author cocitation: A literature measure of intellectual structure. *Journal of the American Society for Information Science, 32*(3), 163-171.

White, H. D., & McCain, K. W. (1998). Visualizing a discipline: An author co-citation analysis of information science, 1972-1995. *Journal of the American Society for Information Science, 49*(4), 327.

White, H. D. (2003). Author cocitation analysis and pearson's r. *Journal of the American Society for Information Science and Technology, 54*(13), 1250-1259.

Woodman, R. W. (1989). Organizational change and development: New arenas for inquiry and action. *Journal of Management, 15*(2), 205.

Vita

Lieutenant Brian R. Low graduated from Sky View High School in Smithfield, Utah. He entered undergraduate studies at Utah State University in Logan, Utah where he graduated with a Bachelor of Science degree in Civil Engineering in May 2003; he was also commissioned there through Detachment 860, AFROTC.

His first assignment was to Fairchild AFB, WA, 92nd Civil Engineer Squadron in June 2003. While stationed at Fairchild AFB, WA he served as an Engineering Project Manager and Chief of the Maintenance Engineering section. In August 2005, he entered the Graduate School of Engineering and Management, Air Force Institute of Technology. Upon graduation, he will be assigned to the 355th Civil Engineer Squadron at Davis-Monthan AFB, AZ.

REPORT DOCUMENTATION PAGE

The public reporting burden for this collection of information is estimated to average 1 hour per response, including the time for reviewing instructions, searching existing data sources, gathering and maintaining the data needed, and completing and reviewing the collection of information. Send comments regarding this burden estimate or any other aspect of the collection of information, including suggestions for reducing this burden to Department of Defense, Washington Headquarters Services, Directorate for Information Operations and Reports (0704-0188), 1215 Jefferson Davis Highway, Suite 1204, Arlington, VA 22202-4302. Respondents should be aware that notwithstanding any other provision of law, no person shall be subject to an penalty for failing to comply with a collection of information if it does not display a currently valid OMB control number.
PLEASE DO NOT RETURN YOUR FORM TO THE ABOVE ADDRESS.

1. REPORT DATE *(DD-MM-YYYY)* 16-02-2007	2. REPORT TYPE **Master's Thesis**	3. DATES COVERED *(From – To)* Sep 2005 – Mar 2007

4. TITLE AND SUBTITLE Mapping Change Management: A Co-citation Analysis	5a. CONTRACT NUMBER
	5b. GRANT NUMBER
	5c. PROGRAM ELEMENT NUMBER
6. AUTHOR(S) Low, Brian R., 1st Lieutenant, USAF	5d. PROJECT NUMBER
	5e. TASK NUMBER
	5f. WORK UNIT NUMBER

7. PERFORMING ORGANIZATION NAMES(S) AND ADDRESS(S) Air Force Institute of Technology Graduate School of Engineering and Management (AFIT/EN) 2950 Hobson Way WPAFB OH 45433-7765	8. PERFORMING ORGANIZATION REPORT NUMBER AFIT/GEM/ENV/07-M8
9. SPONSORING/MONITORING AGENCY NAME(S) AND ADDRESS(ES) n/a	10. SPONSOR/MONITOR'S ACRONYM(S)
	11. SPONSOR/MONITOR'S REPORT NUMBER(S)

12. DISTRIBUTION/AVAILABILITY STATEMENT
APPROVED FOR PUBLIC RELEASE; DISTRIBUTION UNLIMITED.

13. SUPPLEMENTARY NOTES

14. ABSTRACT
  Today's organizations are continually undergoing changes to make improvements in their efficiency and effectiveness. The ability for organizations to effectively implement and sustain successful change, however, has been limited, with most change initiative failing to attain the desired success.   To counter this trend, researchers, across several disciplines, have worked to provide practitioners better insight into how to facilitate change within their organizations. This research has developed many theories as to what constitutes and how best to implement change, but lacks a unifying theory that encompasses all aspects of change research.
  This effort took a step in providing a better understanding of the change management field and its nature. By using a co-citation methodology, 141 influential authors from the field of change management were identified. Using quantitative techniques, their works were categorized into identifiable sub-groups within the field and mapped, providing insight into the level of integration that has occurred within the field and across the disciplines that have explored change. Also, the extent that the existing theories have began to converge toward a unifying theory is observed. The culmination of this effort was to provide future researchers better direction in what research needs to be done, to help the field of change mature towards a unifying theory. This unifying theory can then be translated into successful practices that can enable organizations to successful transition thorough needed change initiatives.

15. SUBJECT TERMS
  change management, co-citation, convergence, research integration

16. SECURITY CLASSIFICATION OF:			17. LIMITATION OF ABSTRACT	18. NUMBER OF PAGES	19a. NAME OF RESPONSIBLE PERSON Lt Col Daniel T. Holt
REPORT U	ABSTRACT U	c. THIS PAGE U	UU	141	19b. TELEPHONE NUMBER *(Include area code)* 785-3636 x7396 daniel.holt@afit.edu